IMPROVISING REAL LIFE

Personal Story in Playback Theatre

IMPROVISING REAL LIFE

Personal Story in Playback Theatre

20th Anniversary Edition

Jo Salas

Tusitala Publishing

Improvising Real Life: Personal Story in Playback Theatre.
20th Anniversary Edition.

Published by Tusitala Publishing,
137 Hasbrouck Road, New Paltz, NY 12561.
www.tusitalapublishing.com

First published in 1993 by Kendall/Hunt Publishing Company,
Dubuque, Iowa.
Second edition (Kendall/Hunt) 1996.
Third edition (Tusitala) 1999.
Fourth edition 2013.

Frontispiece from a drawing by Ann E. Hale.
Cover art by the author.
Cover design by Linda Engler.
Back cover photo by Caylena Cahill, www.caylena.com.
Author photo by Linda Engler.

Library of Congress Card Catalogue Number: 99-071307
ISBN—978-0-9642350-9-0

Printed in the United States of America.
5 4 3 2 1

For Michael Clemente, Playback actor

no words for what he gave us
and how much we miss him

Meaning is at the core of the creative process and of storytelling. It is both the goal and the attribute. When it is our own life story we are telling or a story from our lives, we become aware that we are not the victims of random and chaotic circumstances, that we, too, despite our grief or feelings of insignificance, are living meaningfully in a meaningful universe. And, again, the response to our own story, as well as to the stories of others, is "Yes. Yes, I have a story. Yes, I exist."

— Deena Metzger, *Writing for Your Life.*

Contents

Foreword: Who has the next story?

The bus from Istanbul pulls off the ferry and into the sleepy port of Canakkale, the closest modern town to the site of the Troy of legend. What revelations will this exhumed city choose to share with this pilgrim on a parallel journey to stage yet another adaptation of *The Trojan Women*? I want to address the Second Gulf War. I am looking for patterns in the history of violence on the very battleground of one of the oldest wars ever written about, in a country that borders today's Iraq. Closer to the site, the replica of a wooden horse towers above the tree line. I want to get past it and the visitor's center, walk across the thick city walls, touch the stones, stand right there where Hecuba's cries were heard, while Cassandra's warnings were not.

For the entire day I am Troy's lone visitor. Wandering alone at the site is almost magical. The experience is as rich and layered as the place itself, where consecutive cities were built, destroyed, and rebuilt time and again. As I take in the place, something soon becomes puzzlingly clear: how could the site be so small? Standing on the heights of the Temple of Athena, it is easy to picture Achilles running around the city walls taunting the locals into a good fight. Homer's description takes on a historical dimension. Troy offers its first revelation: by contrast to its size, the story of what happened here assumes even larger proportions. The scorched deposit of earth and debris named "Troy VII" tells its own tale. Indeed something quite dramatic occurred on this layer, which coincides with the time when historians place the violent conflict immortalized in the *Iliad*. But no pile of burnt stone could ever stand up against the epic nature and enduring power of the human story.

With copious notes, hundreds of photos, and a handful of dirt, I set off for Smyrna, the birthplace of Homer, a few hours down the coast. During an unscheduled stop at a town nestled below rocky hills called Bergama, I find something that I am not looking for. Something much more significant.

Bergama is the name given in Turkey to the Hellenic Pergamon of lore, a city that for almost two centuries was considered the most cultured and progressive of the realm, rivaling Athens and Alexandria. It was also home to the most important sanatorium of its time. Standing at the center of the Asklepion, the ancient healing center once run by the renowned Galen, I notice the unmistakable shape of an amphitheatre as part of the building complex. A much larger one stands next to the acropolis, so this one must have been used for something different. Along with techniques that included the interpretation of patients' dreams and the use of music, theatre was at the heart of the famed therapy offered at the Asklepion. I remember the quote from Lao Tzu I keep on my desk at home: "A good traveler has no fixed plans and is not intent on arriving." I am moved by this unexpected gift offered by the journey.

I had travelled to Turkey with the goal of finding ancient patterns relating to human violence and the stories told about it in a field of deep time, but an improvised stop had rewarded me with something more meaningful. Somewhere almost exactly halfway between the place of the mythical story and the home of the mythical storyteller, I had stumbled upon an ancient site where the telling of stories, as intimate and humble as someone's dreams, or as large as would befit a theatre built for hundreds, was a recognized healing practice. In one of the birthplaces of theatre, I had found a different ancient pattern, one that I could build upon. My journey revealed a deeper purpose, and this newfound awareness has since grounded my practice.

I have learned to look for signs of this tradition wherever my work takes me, and have seldom been left empty-handed. I have seen it in the way the Maxacali people, deep in the Brazilian Amazon, sing and dance their dreams and experiences into consciousness "to make them part of real life" (talking about them won't suffice). I have seen it among survivors of the ongoing conflict in Colombia as they declaim, according to the old ways, their personal recollection of violent events with rich lyrical description as well as attention to fact (Colombia is one of the few places in Latin America where these oral traditions are preserved), and I have seen it also in the practice of Playback Theatre, a form that has struck a chord with communities throughout the world. Indeed, its global appeal is a telling sign that it is time to recognize that Playback has long entered into a place that only transformative practices reach. It has fulfilled a need for the expression of personal stories, showing a malleability that allows for the recognition of that which is most specific to our sense of self, while at the same time embracing, with deceptive simplicity, performative principles that run deep and ring true across cultural difference.

Improvising Real Life is doing its part. The first volume on the form, it describes with great clarity and accessibility the history and principles that shape it. Translated into at least eight languages, it continues to play a central role in planting the seeds for the spread and understanding of Playback Theatre from San Francisco to Tokyo, from Kabul to Buenos Aires. Written by one of its founders, it offers to the uninitiated, the student, and the practitioner, a unique perspective and context relating to its birth, intended purpose, discoveries, and meanings. Years of accumulated experiences have resulted in revisions that give this edition a renewed relevance. Yet, after we acknowledge the above, we must look into its deeper layers—as in the site of Troy—not only for reflections and valuable tips on Playback's theory and practices, but for its insights into something much larger: a unique point of view into the nature of theatre itself, that is to say, on what theatre can reveal to us about what makes us human.

As it sews together memory, reflection, and disciplinary rigor, *Improvising Real Life* reveals that not only the whole world can be a stage, but so can every person. We too are like arenas upon which dramas are played, and while parting the curtains on our private moments is risky business, the perspective afforded to the brave is life affirming. Conducted by skilled artists, the ritual aesthetics of Playback transform the personal into the shared in ways that can lead to deeper understandings. If self is a symbolic construct, perhaps it will be best built in the creative company of trusted others, one song, one story at a time.

Jo Salas has been speaking to us from the pages of this book for twenty years, a sort of voyage unto itself, at a critical time of soul searching and transformation, straddling the millennium. The ancient Greeks called their storytellers *rhapsodes*, "those who sew songs together." They represented them with cloak and walking stick, exactly the same way as they depicted the traveller. These were the first to sing, from memory and improvisation, the epic poems later known as the *Iliad*, but also simple news from places visited. Both story and journey are often rich and interchangeable metaphors for life. But a life, a story, or a journey may not reveal much until they are sung, and the supporting structures are revealed. Engaging in this task will show meaning in chaos, openings at dead ends, turning points where lives are tested, and in connecting them, send us on a path with a measure of direction. Learning to recognize these invisible patterns in their infinite yet specific possibilities, not just in us but also in others, is a real life's work. A life affirmed, not hampered, by our ability to take creative risks, to open up, to have the next story to share with others in a treasured moment. A life not bound by oppressive structures but liberated by expressive ones.

Roberto G. Varea,
Co-founder, Performing Arts and Social Justice Program,
University of San Francisco
Steering Committee Member, Theatre Without Borders

Introduction

This book describes a form of improvisation that is based on stories of ordinary and not-so-ordinary life events told during a performance—dreams, memories, fantasies, tragedies, farces: all holographic glimpses into the lives of real people. It is accessible and fun, and yet carries dimensions of depth and sophistication. It takes place in theatres, but also outside them—it can work in virtually any setting, because by its nature it adapts to the needs and concerns of whoever is present. Whether in the hands of polished performers or awkward beginners, Playback Theatre celebrates individual experience, and the connections between people—their collective experience—through their stories.

People who are drawn to practice Playback usually find themselves doing it for its own rewards—the fun of it, the satisfaction of bringing a story to life and knowing that you have given a memorable gift to a stranger, or perhaps to a friend. Other kinds of rewards—money, recognition, prestige—are not so easy to come by through something that defies categorization the way Playback Theatre does. It is artistic, healing, community-building, visionary, all at the same time. It is, perhaps, a kind of synthesis of these functions that has not been familiar in our culture for hundreds of years.

I have written this book most of all as a resource for the many people now doing Playback, and for those who would like to learn more about it. As someone who teaches Playback Theatre to new and experienced people, I know that it's not something you can really learn from a book. What I'm offering will be, I hope, a supplement to hands-on training, a supportive and informative companion.

Chapter 1 tells about the beginnings of Playback Theatre

—when, where, and how it arose—and about the path of the original Playback Theatre company. Chapter 2 discusses the sense of story, the aesthetic and psychological basis of the work. Chapter 3 describes the different forms with which we can respond to an audience member's story. Chapter 4 is about the issues, challenges, and pleasures of Playback acting. In chapter 5, we look at the complex role of the conductor, or emcee. Chapter 6 deals with music in Playback Theatre, how this integral element can help to mold the scenes and support the actors. Chapter 7 explores the essential framework of presentation and ritual in a theatre where the content itself is always unexpected. Chapter 8 focuses on Playback's healing aspects, both in therapeutic settings and in more general contexts. In chapter 9 we see how Playback can fit into many different corners of the community. And in chapter 10, we extend this exploration out to the world, looking at Playback in different countries to see how it changes, how it stays the same.

What I see and say about Playback Theatre is from my own particular vantage point, which is not precisely the same as anyone else's. It's important to say this, especially when talking about a work that above all attends to and honors subjective experience. Playback Theatre has been an integral part of my life since 1975. I helped to start the original company, and have been connected, as teacher, guest performer, friend, compatriot, with many of the groups and individuals who have since become involved in Playback Theatre. I am very aware of how the work has changed and adapted itself, and that my way, our way, is not the only or right way to do Playback Theatre. So this book is not meant to establish an orthodoxy. Playback is far too dynamic and mercurial for me or anyone else to capture and freeze in print. However, I believe that it is valuable for there to be a description of Playback Theatre in its more or less original form, as a point of reference for those embarking on their own journeys of exploration. And there are certain basic values and practices which remain constant through all permutations, without which the work becomes something else, not Playback. These qualities will, I hope, become apparent in the following pages.

The stories that illustrate the book have been drawn from real stories told in performances, workshops, and rehearsals. Some have been adapted slightly according to the needs of the chapter in which they appear. I have changed the names of all tellers, actors, and conductors to preserve their privacy. Apart from Jonathan Fox's, the only real names I have used are the directors whose first and last names appear in chapters 5, 8, and 10.

1

The Beginnings

"Who has the next story?"

The man asking the question is the conductor, or emcee, of a Playback Theatre performance. Behind him on the low stage are five actors, two women and three men, dressed in plain dark-colored pants and tops, sitting expectantly on wooden boxes. One of them has just finished portraying a sea gull; another a New York City cop. But now they are onstage as themselves, until the next scene. A musician sits to one side, surrounded by an eclectic assortment of instruments.

Two people in the audience raise their hands. The conductor gestures to one.

"I saw you first," he says, smiling regretfully at the other. A young man comes to the stage and sits beside the conductor.

"Hi!" says the conductor. "Your name is...?"

"Gary," says the young man. There's a look of humorous intelligence in his eyes.

"Welcome to the teller's chair, Gary. Where does your story take place?"

"Well, two places, I guess. I work for the gas company— I'm a ditch digger. But every three weeks I go and spend a weekend at St Catherine's College, in the city. I'm getting my bachelor's degree. It's a program for people like me who can't take time off work to go to school. So we have these very packed weekends, and then lots of homework."

"Can you pick one of the actors to be you?"

Gary looks at the actors carefully. He points to one. "Sorry, I can't remember your name. Can you be me?" The actor nods and stands.

"Who else is important in your story?"

"Well, the story's really about a woman in the program called Eugenia. She inspires me, I guess. She's so alive, and I know she's dealing with much harder things than I am. She comes from Jamaica, and she's still getting used to this culture, and she has a young child. But she's always so energetic and enthusiastic. She's really smart, too. I feel good just talking to her."

Gary chooses someone else to play Eugenia. There are a few more questions and answers. Then "Watch!" says the conductor.

The lights are lowered. Music begins. In the dimness, the actors silently place boxes around the stage. Some of them costume themselves in pieces of cloth. The music stops and the lights go up. The scene unfolds. The teller's story is there, crafted with movement, dialogue and music. The actors bring out Gary's own energy and enthusiasm and courage as he goes to class with Eugenia. The scene honors his vision of a life beyond digging ditches.

Sitting onstage beside the conductor, Gary watches his story come to life. For the audience, the emotions that cross his face are part of the drama. The scene comes to a close. The actors turn to the teller, their gesture making a gift to him of what they have just done.

The conductor asks Gary to comment. "Is that how it is?" He nods. "Yes, pretty much."

"Gary, thank you for your story. And good luck!"

He returns to his seat, smiling. Another teller comes to the stage, and another. One story follows another like variegated beads on a string. There is a thread holding them together, hidden but palpable.

Playback Theatre is an original form of theatrical improvisation in which people tell real events from their lives, then watch them enacted on the spot. Playback Theatre often takes place in performance settings, with a trained company of actors enacting the stories of audience members; or the occasion may be the meeting of a private group, where members become the actors for each other's stories. There is a clear format, though it is constantly adapted in a variety of ways. Any life experience may be told and enacted in Playback Theatre, from the mundane to the transcendent, the hilarious to the tragic—and some stories may be all of these. The process is effective at almost any level of skill on the part of the actors. All that is needed is respect, empathy, and playfulness. On the other hand, especially for those working with Playback in performance, there is also room for great sophistication and artistry.

The name "Playback Theatre" refers both to the form itself and to groups that practice this work. There are by now many Playback groups around the world, and if they call themselves "Playback Theatre" (not all of them do) they also add a name that will distinguish them from other companies—usually the name of their city or region. There is Sydney Playback Theatre, London Playback Theatre, Playback Theatre Northwest, and so on.

The basic idea of Playback Theatre is very simple. And yet its implications are complex and profound. When people are brought together and invited to tell personal stories to be acted out, there are a number of messages and values that are communicated, many of which are radically at odds with the prevailing messages of our culture. One is the idea that you, your personal experience, is *worthy* of this kind of attention. We are saying that your life is a fit subject for art, that others may find your story interesting, may learn from it, be moved by it. We are saying that we can look closer to home than the cultural icons of Hollywood and Broadway to find reflections that can bring meaning to our world. We are also saying that effective artistic expression is not the exclusive province of the professional performer; that all of us, even you, even I, may be able to reach into ourselves, or out of ourselves, to create a thing of beauty that can touch other hearts. We are saying that *story* itself is of the profoundest importance, that we need stories to construct meaning in our lives, and that our lives themselves are full of stories, if we can learn to discern them. We are saying that there is more—and less—to theatre than the great plays of our heritage, that before and alongside the tradition of literary theatre there has always been a theatre that is more immediate, more personal, more humble, more accessible, and that this theatre grows out of the undying need for connection through aesthetic ritual.[1]

Linked as it is to ancient and non-technological theatre traditions, Playback Theatre is also new. It is a product of our times, growing out of contemporary currents and seeking to address contemporary needs. Where did it come from?

Playback Theatre began as the vision of Jonathan Fox, and here I am going to be telling you some of my own story, because as Jonathan's wife and professional partner, I was part of Playback's birth.

In 1974, we were living in New London, Connecticut, a small coastal town shadowed by a cluster of grim industries. Jonathan was working as a writer and part-time college English instructor. We had several friends whose children attended a small experimental school. They asked Jonathan to help them develop a theatre piece that they would perform for their children. Although he wasn't actively involved in theatre, any one who knew Jonathan knew his theatrical, clowny expressiveness, his taste for spectacle, and the way

---

[1]Some of these points, and others that I will be making in this book, are explored in more theoretical depth in Jonathan Fox's *Acts of Service: Spontaneity, Commitment, Tradition in the Nonscripted Theatre* (New Paltz, NY: Tusitala, 1994).

he could be entertaining and inclusive and respectful all at the same time.

Jonathan had been interested in theatre since childhood. But he had been discouraged by the competitive, sometimes narcissistic aspects of the world of mainstream theatre. Instead, he had found his models and inspiration in the values and aesthetics of very early oral traditions, in the current alternative theatres, and in the essential, redeeming roles of ritual and storytelling in the pre-industrial village life of rural Nepal, where he had spent two years as a Peace Corps volunteer. There he saw some parallels to the western legacy of medieval mystery and miracle plays he had studied at Harvard. These plays were informal, attuned to the cycles of the seasons and the holidays, intimate, and unashamedly amateur.

When the theatre project with the parents in New London was over, everyone wanted to go on working together. They invited me to be their musician. I was pleased—and apprehensive. Although I had played music all my life, I didn't know how to improvise, how to play without written music in front of me. It was the beginning of a long process of unlearning and re-learning for me, of searching for my long lost spontaneity and fluency in music.

We called ourselves "It's All Grace." We performed on beaches, on the lawn at an institution for retarded people, in a church basement. Our shows were improvisationally developed, thematically profound, and ritualistic, with much energy and a certain amount of anarchy. It was exciting and rewarding in many ways. But Jonathan was still searching.

One day, over a cup of hot chocolate in a diner, the idea came to him: an improvisational theatre based simply on the real-life stories of people in the audience, enacted on the spot by a team of actors.

Some members of It's All Grace were eager to move in

this new direction. Together we experimented with what it meant to make theatre out of our own personal stories, with no more preparation than our spontaneity could give us in the moment. We did one show. Crude as it was, the process worked.

In August of 1975, Jonathan and I moved from New London to New Paltz in upstate New York, three hours away. It was a hard goodbye. Jonathan had been offered the opportunity to complete his psychodrama training at the Moreno Institute in Beacon, NY, training he hoped would give him the courage and wisdom to fully face any audience story, no matter how delicate or painful.

By November of that year, we had found another group of people to join us in exploring the new theatre. Most of them came through the psychodrama network, people who were attracted to the intimacy and intensity of enacting real-life stories. Some had been involved in conventional theatre, some had not. Between them, they brought a rich variety of life experience. As the work developed, we came to realize more and more the importance of such a variety of personality, age, social class, career, cultural background, and theatre experience. As with the performers of mystery plays, it was an asset to have ordinary people as actors.

Zerka Moreno, the widow of psychodrama's founder J.L. Moreno and worldwide leader of the psychodrama movement, was intrigued by our ideas and intentions and generous enough to pay the rent of our rehearsal space for that first year. Even in its early stages, she saw the affinity between our work and Moreno's inspirational spontaneity theatre, from which had developed classical psychodrama.

One evening, we sat around the oilcloth-covered dining table at the Moreno Institute, drinking tea and looking for a name for this collective adventure. Names flew around the table, some inspired, some pretentious, some obscure, some witty. We filtered out all but a few, and in true psychodrama fashion, we role-reversed with each one of them. How do you feel, Name, about representing this thing we're doing? There was one name which revealed itself to be the right one: Playback Theatre.

Playback Theatre's first five years were a time of great excitement and great confusion. Often we felt that we were groping in the dark, guided only by the glimmer of a vision. We stumbled on refinements that worked, and they became part of our form. We learned how to listen deeply and how to find the courage to act not knowing for sure if we would get it "right." We learned the importance of a ritual frame in which to weave our ephemeral stories, a frame of familiar, consistent elements such as the sequence of acting out a story and the physical set-up of the stage. We worked hard on our connections to each other, knowing that our theatre depended on our intuitive teamwork. Some of the earliest members drifted away, leaving us with a core of people who have remained to this day. Others joined over the years, through auditions that we tried to make as human and enjoyable as possible.

Our first performances were simply open rehearsals. Well aware of our lack of polish, we invited people to explore with us, to play our warm-up games with us, and to tell stories together. Gradually we felt ready to present our performances more formally: now there was an admission fee, an audience, and a team that felt like a team on the other side of the footlights. But we never built the fourth wall. Throughout our performances, audience members joined us on stage, and actors resumed their own identities between roles.

In 1977 we moved away from the church hall in Beacon and the supportive closeness of the Moreno Institute to the Mid-Hudson Arts and Science Center in Poughkeepsie, our home for the next nine years. We established a regular "First

Friday" performance series. Each month there would be new faces, and each month we would also see people who came faithfully for our "theatre of neighbors, not strangers," as Jonathan often described it in his introduction. And although some of the audience might have been strangers when they walked in, the telling of stories led indeed to a feeling of shared humanity. People could watch a fellow audience member's story come to life on the stage and think: "That could be me."

Some audience members, seeing what happened when people were invited to tell their stories in this gentle, respectful, and artistic context, asked us to come and do Playback Theatre at their places of work. We began to perform in the community. We went to a pediatrics ward where sick children, some wheeled in on their beds, told of their operations, their accidents, their feelings. We performed at a riverside festival, making our entrance by clambering down a hillside playing percussion instruments. We leapt up between speeches at a conference on the future of Dutchess County, giving the audience a chance to express their responses to what they were hearing.

In 1979, a man from Australia saw our performance at a psychodrama conference in New York City. He wanted to know if we would come to Australia—yes, we would, if he could arrange and pay for it. The next year, four of us travelled to New Zealand and Australia. We led workshops and presented performances in Auckland, Wellington, Sydney, and Melbourne. Since we needed more than four people for a performance, our idea was to recruit workshop members from each center to join us as a Playback team. It worked. The selection process was challenging, for us as well as for the workshop participants, but in each place we ended up with a wonderful "company." And the audience was able to relate to us in a different and more intimate way than if we had only been the American visitors.

Performing with local actors also helped with occasional linguistic difficulties. Even though we all spoke English, tellers would sometimes use an idiom that had never crossed the Pacific. The American actors were stumped by one dramatic story about a "chook" until their Aussie counterparts enlightened them—a chook is a chicken.

The trip was a turning point. The Australians and New Zealanders in our workshops responded strongly to Playback Theatre. In each place, some continued to work together, forming Playback companies which have since developed their own momentum and distinctive styles. For the first time, Playback was more than our own group. In the years since 1980, this process has continued. Now, in 1993, there are people doing Playback theatre in about 17 countries around the world, as well as across the United States. They are working in theatres, schools, clinics, businesses, prisons—anywhere that there are people with stories to tell.

Our company, becoming known as the "original Playback Theatre" to distinguish it from the other companies being formed, continued to grow and change throughout the eighties. We did a great deal of social service work—with the elderly, at-risk youth, handicapped people, people in prisons. We strove to develop ourselves artistically, knowing that the more skilled we were the more deeply we could serve the story. We experimented with bringing some prepared material into our shows, alternating rehearsed scenes with audience stories on a set theme, such as love, or nuclear war. In almost every show, we invited audience members to trade places with the actors and act out a story. The spontaneity of the audience actors, their "beginner's mind," was often the high point of the evening. Sometimes we found novel ways to involve the audience. In one show where the theme of birth had emerged strongly, a dozen men from the audience came on stage and, one by one, presented themselves in the role of a woman experiencing some aspect of pregnancy, childbirth, and early motherhood—a farcical first visit to the obstetrician, the physical trials of pregnancy, a magical moment nursing a baby in a sleeping house.

We found ourselves in demand as workshop leaders, often with people who were more interested in experiencing this work for their own growth than in becoming professional Playback actors. We offered children's classes, and saw the freshness and insight that children, including our own, could bring to Playback Theatre.

For some of us, Playback Theatre became a job. There were grants that paid us salaries, meager and unreliable as they might have been. We rented an office and hired an administrator. We had a board of directors, and a budget, and a growing set of worries. By the late 1980's, we were tired. We all still loved the stories, and after many years together we were part of each others' lives. But we were running out of energy to get together each week, to organize performances, to generate enough money to meet the budget. We decided, painfully, to stop. At least, to end our schedule as it had developed, to let go of our office and our administrator, and to see what happened. We did what we knew would be our last "First Friday." Two women in the audience, Playback regulars, cried when I sang "The Carnival Is Over."

But it wasn't over. Playback Theatre, the form we created, has grown steadily as more and more people experience its simple power. Some of us from the original group now work with other groups, at home and around the world. And we still perform as a company, when we want to, when an invitation piques our interest. We have gone back to grass roots, finding again something like the simplicity of our first years.

Meanwhile, Playback Theatre as a form continues to evolve and develop. New contexts bring new ideas and innovations, some of which have a lasting influence, some that are experimental and shortlived. Through the International Playback Theatre Network, Playback practitioners hear of what others across the globe are doing and may be inspired themselves. The essence remains the same: a theatre based on the spontaneous enactment of personal stories.

2

The Sense of Story

The Story Must Be Told

At a summer training workshop, I watched Playback actors from all over the world improvising stories together. There were Australians with energetic movements and loud voices, Russians using metaphor and silence, Europeans speaking sparse poetic dialogue, Americans acting from the heart. The Playback scenes that I saw were often far removed in style from our original work. And yet it was evident that, even with all this variation, the Playback Theatre process worked—*as long as the story was told.* It didn't matter so much if the scene was done skillfully or clumsily, with dialogue, in movement, realistically, impressionistically, with influences from commedia dell'arte or traditional Russian theatre. If the story was told, the scene was a success, the teller was moved, the audience satisfied. If it wasn't, theatrical brilliance couldn't help.

In these workshop scenes, it wasn't always told. Sometimes it was lost in unnecessary details, or in confused communication between the actors, or in someone's need for the limelight. Sometimes a symbolic enactment became meaninglessly remote from concrete experience. I started to pay close attention to what the successful enactments had in common. It seemed to me that underlying all other considerations there were two essential elements, functioning together like the cup and the empty space inside it: an intuitive feeling for the meanings of the teller's experience, and an aesthetic sense of story itself.

Everyone on the Playback team—the actors, the conductor, the musician, the lighting person if there is one—needs to be a storyteller. They need to be able to conjure the shape of a story, and they must be able to fit this template onto the teller's sometimes ragged account. If they don't, everyone feels somehow cheated—the teller, the audience, even the actors themselves. But if they do, there's a palpable sense of delight and satisfaction. We are deeply affirmed when we see a piece of life shaped in this way.

The Need For Stories

How do we know what a story is? We know because we're surrounded by stories from the beginning of life. We know that a story has to begin somewhere, to tell how things were to start with. Then there has to be some kind of development, or surprise, or turning, and then an end, a place to leave it. There are infinite possibilities of scale and shape, from the suggestive subtlety of a one-minute fable to the massive contours of a Victorian novel. It is the presence of form, meaning, elements in relation to each other, that tells us: this is a story.

The form of a story is so basic and so pervasive that children from the age of one or two can recognize it when they hear it. And as any parent or teacher or babysitter or big sister can tell you, children want to hear stories. In fact, we never grow out of it—we all *want* to hear stories, and we seek them out wherever they are offered—in the movies, in novels, in the newspaper, in gossip overheard on the train.

And we learn to tell our own. We must, in order to survive. Life while it is happening to us can seem random and undirected. It's often only when we tell the story of what happened that some order can emerge from the abundant jumble of details and impressions. When we weave our experience into stories, we find meaning in what we have undergone.

18

Telling our stories to others helps us to integrate the story's meaning for us personally. It is a way, too, for us to contribute to the universal quest for meaning. The intrinsic element of *form* in a story can transmute chaos and restore a sense of belonging to a world that is fundamentally purposeful after all. Even the most desperately painful of experiences are in some way redeemed when they are told as stories. Think of the unforgettable stories of Holocaust survivors, how both the teller and the reader, or listener, grow from the telling.

When the Need Is Not Met

People who for some reason cannot tell their story are at a terrible disadvantage. We *need* to be heard, to be affirmed and welcomed as one who shares the human condition. And we need to make sense of our existence. In *The Man Who Mistook His Wife For a Hat*, Oliver Sacks describes a man with Korsakov's syndrome. The illness has destroyed his memory so that he is condemned to live in the present, cut off from all sense of antecedents to his situation, desperately struggling to hold onto events around him long enough to form them into stories. Sacks writes:

> Each of us *is* a singular narrative, which is con-structed, continually, unconsciously, by, through, and in us—through our perceptions, our feelings, our thoughts; and, not least, our discourse, our spoken narrations....To be ourselves, we must *have* ourselves—possess, if need be re-possess, our life-stories.[1]

---

[1] Oliver Sacks, *The Man Who Mistook His Wife for a Hat*, (New York: Harper and Row, 1987), 100-111.

I often take part in Playback Theatre performances for emotionally disturbed children in residential treatment. The children, ages five to fourteen, are eager to come to these shows, and use them to tell important experiences—getting adopted, the death of a sister, playing with some children at the park and feeling for a little while that you are part of their family. The only problem we have is that their desire to tell is so strong that we always end up disappointing the ones who don't get a chance to be tellers. There might be ten hands waving in the air: "Pick me! Pick me!" But there's never enough time to enact everyone's story.

It is poignant to see this fierce yearning to be heard. For when else in their lives do they have such an opportunity? In a busy institution full of troubled kids there are very few times that a staff member can listen attentively to one child's story. Few, if any, of the children have the patience or maturity to listen to each other. And most have come from families where concrete survival needs like food, shelter, and physical safety have preempted the subtler hunger for story.

Unlike Sacks' patient, these children and many other deprived people remember their stories. They are aware that telling them is of urgent importance. What they lack is the opportunity that most of us have to share stories in the course of our daily lives.

Everyday Stories

What is happening when we tell each other our stories? We start with the fundamental need to communicate something that has happened to us, something we have seen or experienced or realized. We sense that telling it to others may bring completion. Our sense of story comes into play. We do our best to shape our perceptions and memories. Based on our feeling of what it is about, of why this story calls to be told, we choose to include some details and omit others, we emphasize this point and skim over that one. We know, more or less, when the story should begin and end, and what the heart of it is.

This everyday storytelling doesn't always come easily. Sometimes our story is so buried it seems inaccessible. Or, confused about the point of the story, we stumble around in a thicket of details. Some people are just more gifted as storytellers than others. We all have friends who can be spellbinding even when telling about mundane things, and others who are boring and hard to follow no matter what the content of their story.

My friend is telling me about something that has just happened at work: "I was in the middle of teaching a class today when suddenly we saw a huge hot-air balloon landing right outside on the playground. We rushed outside, all the teachers and kids. God, we were all so excited! The balloonists climbed out and said that something had gone wrong and they'd had to make an emergency landing. Then the assistant principal came out. He was unbelievable—he told them this was state property and they had no right to be there and he would call the police if they didn't leave immediately."

She instinctively shaped her account like a story. She didn't tell me every single detail of what had happened, only the features that would give me the most vivid picture of what she had experienced.

The stories we tell about ourselves accumulate into a sense of self, an identity, the most personal of mythologies. We also tell stories about our world, and they help us to comprehend what otherwise might seem to be a confusing and random universe. History, myth, and legend are all bodies of stories that have this function. They are ways of

21

organizing and accounting for human experience so that it can be understood and remembered.

Stories in Playback Theatre

We are, all of us, storytellers. Story is built into our way of thought. We need stories for our emotional health and our sense of place in the world. All our lives we seek opportunities to hear and tell them. I'm convinced that this is the reason that Playback Theatre has grown the way it has: it is a place where the need for story is fed.

"Can I tell something just really ordinary?" asks a college student after a dramatic enactment of a nightmare. Her story is about going to a spa with her mother and having a mud bath for the first time. The conductor's questions bring out further dimensions. The girl's mother lives far away. This moment takes place during one of their rare, treasured times together. The teller chooses women for all the roles, including the mud itself and the friendly attendant. The enactment takes on the aura of a female rite; the mothering, nurturing experience of being immersed in elemental mud, being soothed and warmed.

In Playback Theatre our job is to go further than we usually do in everyday storytelling. Our job is to reveal the shapeliness and meaning in any experience, even the ones that are unclear or formless in the telling. We dignify stories with ritual and aesthetic awareness, and link them together so that they form a collective story about a community of people, whether the temporary community of a public audience, or a group of people whose lives are connected in an ongoing way. A group of people who share stories in this way cannot help but feel their connectedness: Playback Theatre is a potent builder of community. We offer a public arena in which the meaning of individual experience expands to become part of a shared sense of purposeful existence. In Playback Theatre people have sometimes told deeply tragic events from their lives. These stories have led to healing not only for them but also for all of us who are present. Watching a stranger's story unfolding, you can feel that it is your own life, your own passion, that you are witnessing, no matter whether you've actually experienced something similar or not. We are connected by emotions and life currents far deeper than the specific details of our individual experience.

I remember a man who told about the death of his wife years before. At the time, he had been unable to be as emotionally present with his young children as he had wanted. In the audience was his son, now a young adult. At the end of the story these two men were in each other's arms, while all of the small audience and all the Playback people shared in their healing tears.

To fulfill Playback Theatre's promise, we must have a strong sense of the aesthetic, flexible contour of a story and know how to create it from whatever we are given by the teller. We must be able to provide the essential beginning, turning, and conclusion, even when the teller's account doesn't give these to us clearly. We must be alive to the touches that will endow the story with vividness and grace. We need to edit as we improvise, deciding in the moment which of all the features we have heard are essential for the story to be told. We must ask ourselves "Why this story? Why here and now?" in order to feel its inmost meanings.

The Essence of the Story

Finding the heart of the story is a subtle task. You can't just solve it and baldly state it like the solution to a puzzle. You can't reduce it to its essence like a chemical formula.

Whatever the essence is, it *needs* the features of the story to express itself. It is a core of related meanings inseparable from the events themselves, without which the story would not ask to be told.

Sometimes the fullest meaning of a story lies beyond the words spoken—in the teller's facial expression and body language, for example. Once in a Playback Theatre rehearsal a man told a story about a horrible trip to the dentist when he was a child. The story seemed to be about behaving like a "good boy" even when he was full of fear and pain. But when, as the conductor, I asked him who had gone with him to the dentist, he turned full-face to me and his eyes shone. "My father!" he said. That change in his posture and facial expression told me that this story might also be about the closeness between him and his father, who had died long ago. This insight into the story didn't mean that our enactment should then especially focus on Seth's relationship with his father. The richness and effectiveness, not only for the teller but for everyone, comes from allowing all of its dimensions of meaning to be there, echoing and illumining each other.

The Larger Story

Most people come to Playback Theatre with a lifetime's experience of telling and listening to personal stories of all kinds. Once they understand what this theatre is, it seems familiar. "Oh, something that really happened to me," they nod. And yet it's also quite different. Telling your story in a public context, however informal, isn't the same as talking to a friend on the phone. There is the circle of audience and actors, there is the empty space on the stage, and the framework of ritual. These elements transform the field in which stories are told. Like singing in an echoing cave instead of in your living-room, there is an extension of resonance. Tellers usually sense this and respond by telling strong stories, stories that express a piece of their truth, embodied in vivid subjective experience. They bear witness, offering their personal story to the social realm.

Then there are tellers who don't seem to have access to deep stories. They get up and tell mere anecdotes, or "me too" echoes of another teller's story. Or they are confused about what they want to tell and cannot respond to the conductor's attempts to help them clarify. In our company, we used to feel frustrated about such tellers, even angry at them for denying us the satisfaction of enacting a "good" story.

But over time, we've realized that there is always a larger story being told, one that transcends the story of any individual teller. It's the story of this particular event, and everything that happens is part of it, from the time that we gather to the last goodbye. It is mostly the conductor's task to help everyone see this overall story; to remind people of the remarkable fact that we are all here just to honor our stories; to point to the themes that emerge, the connections between stories, the meaning of this person or that person becoming a teller; even, in a problematic performance, to invite the audience to look at our collective responsibility in what is happening. Stories are inseparable from the context of their telling; and the contextual details are as significant as those of the stories themselves.

It's hard, maintaining an awareness of this dimension. Onstage, we tend to focus on the story being told and the challenges of enacting it. We have to keep panning back in our minds like a movie camera to take in the whole picture. The performance is laced with moments that can help us, if we are open to them. One such time comes early in the show. The warm-up phase is over, and the conductor says: "Who is our first teller tonight?" Stillness. Silence. Then there is movement in the audience. A figure detaches itself from the group, comes to the stage, becomes a person with a face, a voice, a name, a story. Every time I witness this I am wonderstruck. How amazing it is that this can happen, that we can say "we are here to enact your story" and a stranger will say "I have a story."

During our Australian tour in 1980 we performed in a rather large and prestigious theatre in Sydney. It was packed, which was gratifying but also, we knew, probably a bad sign in terms of the kinds of stories we could expect. We had learnt by then that the "good" stories, the juicy ones about deep life issues, usually came up when the audience was small or in some way well-connected with each other. People had to have some reason to trust each other. With a big audience in a public show, there was little chance for anything but anecdotes.

And that's what we got in this Sydney show. Stories about possums on the roof, and watching a kookaburra feeding her young. For years we thought of this show as a good example of the superficial level typical of large public performances. But now I think there may have been at least two important dimensions that we failed to be aware of at the time. One was the connection between the theme of the aliens, the wild animals, rudely intruding upon urban lives, and our own visit—we the foreigners, the unknown, suddenly among them. Then there is the totemic nature of the animals themselves. Although it may not be uppermost in a city dweller's awareness, Australia is a land of powerful animal presence. Possums and kookaburras and kangaroos are the heart of the Aboriginal Dreamtime cosmology. Animal stories in Australia must surely be heard in that context.

When a Playback Theatre event begins, we never know what the stories will be, what themes may appear and from where, to be woven into the evening's tapestry. We must awaken our sense of story as we listen to the tellers' words, as we reach for the layers of meaning in our being together in this way, in this time and place.

Elaine's Story

In a public Playback performance, a grey-haired woman called Elaine tells a story about an impromptu naked swim with a much younger man whom she has recently met at a work-shop. The swim is delightful, but when it is time to leave she finds she can't climb out of the pond. The young man helps her by grasping her arms and pulling her out. She finds herself fully, nakedly, face-to-face not only with him but with the uncompromising awareness of her own aging body.

Elaine's description of her experience pointed to its meaning for her. She was amused but obviously not crushed by this embarrassing moment with its echoes of mortality. Instead, she was telling us that she accepted the fact of her aging; she even had some relish for life's way of presenting her with the naked truth.

This story was also part of a larger story. There were significant elements that lay outside, rather than within the story itself, though these two aspects, the content and the context, resonated and commented on each other. The conductor knew Elaine and knew that she was in fact much older than she appeared to be, a seventy-year-old who looked fifty at most. With her permission, he let the audience know this. It made her story even more dramatic. She was the first teller of the evening, which said something about her courage and also her willingness to be seen—both of which were relevant to the story.

The enactment begins with the sightseeing drive which had led up to the swim. The teller's actor (the actor playing

Elaine) is full of high spirits, in contrast to her quieter compan-
ion. The scene builds towards the moment when, heading back
to the workshop, they drive by an inviting-looking pond and
Elaine suggests a swim. "I don't have my bathing suit with me,"
says the young man. "Oh, that's all right, neither do I," says
the teller's actor, exuberantly throwing off the pieces of fabric
she has costumed herself with. They swim and splash in the
cool water. Music conveys their pleasure and abandon. Then
the climax: the young man leaps out effortlessly, but Elaine is
unable to follow. He pulls her up onto the bank. There is a long
moment as they stand there, the young body and the old body.
Elaine's inner experience of that instant is there in the actor's
face and in the accompanying music. Then it is over.

Elaine was one of those tellers who are skilled at presenting their stories. It was not hard for the Playback team to find
an aesthetic form for her tale. Still, they called on their sense
of story to select and shape the key events. They chose to
begin with the sight-seeing drive, knowing that although we
didn't need to see their meeting at the workshop, the story
had to have a beginning, a setting for the main event, as a
range of hills needs the setting of the surrounding plain. When
they got to the climax, the actors stretched the full-frontal
encounter well beyond the actual duration of that moment,
as an outward analogue to Elaine's inner experience. And
then they knew that the story was told. There was no need
to show more, so they ended the scene.

The actors' choices about what to emphasize, what to
omit, came from their collective sense of what this story was
about. From Elaine's words, and from the contextual information I mentioned before, they felt that this was a story
about confronting the fact of aging with grace and a sense of
humor. Their unanimous sense of this meaning, combined
with their sense of story, allowed them to do the scene very

effectively with no discussion or planning. If one of the actors had thought the story was about, for instance, sexual issues between Elaine and the young man, the enactment might have taken a different course, with less artistic unity.

As she watched the scene, Elaine laughed a lot, clasping her hands and leaning in toward the actors. At the end, she turned back to the conductor with a look of satisfaction. "Oh, yes!" she said.

The audience, too, found the story funny. But in the shrieks of laughter at the climax there was also acknowledgment of the depth of that moment. Elaine was not alone in her awareness of time and change, youth and age, spontaneity and rueful limitation.

Finding the interwoven meanings of the teller's experience and rendering them in story form is the heart of the Playback Theatre process. The following chapters will explore each aspect of Playback practice and how it helps in this task.

3

Scenes and Other Forms

A Playback Theatre performance includes several different ways of responding to the stories of the audience. The basic forms developed by the original company are scenes, fluid sculptures, and pairs.[1] We'll look at each of these, and then at some of the other forms that have developed over the years.

Let's say we've come to a public Playback Theatre performance. The audience is made up of some regulars and a number of people here for the first time. The conductor knows that one of her first tasks is to tell the new audience members what Playback is and to show them that it is safe here to tell their stories. For the regulars and newcomers alike, a familiar opening ritual is very important. It underscores the message that the real stories of ordinary people are worthy of public sharing and artistic treatment.

The show begins with some music, followed by action introductions from the performers and a verbal welcome from the conductor, explaining Playback Theatre and setting a mood of warmth and respect.

Fluid Sculptures

It's still not time to launch into stories. The audience needs a way to ease into the Playback process. The company is going to do a series of fluid sculptures—short, abstract aggregates of sound and movement that express audience members' responses to the conductor's questions.

---

[1] Some companies in Australia refer to fluid sculptures and pairs as, respectively, "moments" and "conflicts."

The conductor's first question is an easy one, something that people are likely to want to answer.

"Well, it's Friday night. How do you feel at the end of your work week?"

Three hands go up. The conductor points to one of them. "How about you?"

"Drained. I can't believe I made it through another one."

"OK, and your name is...?"

"Donna."

"Thanks, Donna. Watch."

One actor steps into the middle of the stage. His body seems to wilt as he mutters "It's over...I can't believe it... it's over..." The musician plays slow dissonant chords on the guitar. After a moment, another actor joins the first one, hammering at his head and making shrill non-verbal sounds. Two more actors add their contributions, linking their actions to what's already there, so that by the end there is an organic, kinetic human sculpture that expresses Donna's experience. It's short—no more than a minute from beginning to end.

"Donna, was it that bad?"

"Yes! Thank you."

The conductor is ready to follow up on themes as they present themselves. Since Donna's experience was so grim, she asks if anyone had a different kind of week. Someone says "Better than usual, everything just seemed to flow." This fluid sculpture is completely different from the first one, taking up more space on the stage as the actors translate "flow" into physical terms, accompanied by rather exuberant percussion. There are several more questions, responses, and fluid sculptures, each one a glimpse of a life.

By the time the conductor moves on to the scenes themselves, several things have happened as far as the audience members are concerned. The crux of the Playback process—creating theatre based on real experience—is now apparent to everyone. The audience has seen that they are invited but never pressured to participate. Their responses receive respect and aesthetic attention. They have felt the satisfaction, either directly or vicariously, of recognizing their experience rendered in an artistic form. They have begun to feel their connection to one another, the beginning of a sense of community. And some will have begun to think of other experiences they would like to relate in this context. They are ready to be tellers.

Scenes: The Interview

"We're going to move on now to stories, stories about things that have happened to you, maybe this morning, maybe when you were a child, maybe in a dream." The conductor pauses. "Who is going to be our first teller tonight?"

So far, people have called out responses from their places in the audience. But now it's time for someone to come onstage, to sit in the teller's chair beside the conductor and to tell.

Nothing happens. Some people in the audience glance at each other a little anxiously—what if no one has a story? But the conductor and the actors are relaxed. They know that in this moment of dormancy many stories are ripening. We have only to be patient and one will tumble off the tree.

A man raises his hand, already getting up from his seat. He has come to public performances before but he's never told a story.

"Hi, Leon. You have a story tonight?"

Leon is getting settled in the teller's chair. He looks out at the audience, then back at the conductor.

"Yes, I have a story. It's about my son. And my father."

We are already in the first of the five stages of enacting a story. This stage is the interview. The conductor asks questions to elicit the story. From the beginning, the challenge is to find the clues that will allow the team to make theatre out of raw experience. As we saw in the last chapter, what is needed above all is an understanding of the story's most important meanings, the reason it is being told; and an aesthetic sense of story, without which the scene will lack a coherent and satisfying shape. In the interview, the conductor tries to find out the basic facts of the story—who, where, what happened—as economically as possible. The conductor asks the teller to choose an actor to play himself or herself, and perhaps one or two other key roles. Actors can self-choose other characters, including inanimate elements if they are important to the meaning of the story. As they are picked, the actors stand, inwardly preparing for the role but not yet acting.

"So you and Ivan went to a sweat lodge. Who's going to play you?"

"Andy can be me."

As the actors are chosen, they stand in front of the box they've been sitting on, not acting yet, but listening to the story now with the knowledge that they have a specific role to play. Choosing the actors is very dramatic in itself. There is a visible promise that this conversation between conductor and teller is the preamble to action. The scene-to-be starts to dance in everyone's imagination in the empty space between actors and teller.

The interview comes to an end. Then the conductor's job is over for the time being, and so is the teller's.

"This is Leon's story, about fathering. Let's watch."

The Setting-up

The second stage, the setting-up, takes us into the realm of action. The musician begins to play, improvising music that evokes a contemplative mood. The actors move silently and deliberately into their positions. A couple of them select pieces of cloth as impressionistic costumes or props. Others place boxes around the stage as a simple stage set. There is no discussion.[2] When all are ready, the musician stops and the scene begins.

To the audience it can seem like magic, especially when the scene goes particularly well. How can the actors possibly know what to do without discussion? The secret is that in the absence of a script or a plan of action, the actors depend on their highly developed sense of story, their empathic ability to grasp the layers of meaning in this person's experience, and their openness to each other. The discipline of having to create scenes without verbal planning has honed the skills that they need.

The Enactment

The third stage is the enactment itself.

The scene begins with three of the four actors onstage using movement and sound to evoke the atmosphere of a sweat lodge, an informal Native American tradition where people seek connection and renewal. The musician plays a bamboo flute.

Two of the actors break away to take on their roles as Leon and his little boy Ivan, while the third stands behind them, holding the image of the sweat lodge.

"Daddy, do we have to go?" says the actor playing Ivan, pulling on Leon's arm.

---

[2]In some Playback Theatre companies, actors confer in a huddle before setting up. My observation is that this does not necessarily improve the quality of the scene. Unless you have a significant amount of time to prepare, what you can plan verbally is unlikely to be better than what your intuition and teamwork can come up with. A huddle can also lead to unexpected problems—see chapter 6.

"Remember what I told you?" says Leon gently. "It's going to be special. You and me together. Come on, everyone's waiting for us."

At home later, Leon asks his wife to put the little boy to bed. It's his turn for this nightly ritual, but he's tired.

Ivan is hurt. "I want <u>you</u>, Daddy!"

Leon changes his mind. Snuggling and singing with the boy in the quiet bedroom, he suddenly thinks of his own father, distant from him as a child after divorce took him away to a new family.

Over on stage left, standing on a box in order to be visible to the teller, is the fourth actor, who has self-chosen the role of Leon's father. Leon breaks away from Ivan and joins his own father in a pas-de-deux of memory while the other actors continue to evoke the sleepy bedroom on stage right. The focus goes back and forth between the two elements of the story. The musician is playing a slow but rhythmic chord progression on the guitar.

"When you were little you used to help me wash the car every week," says the father. "Do you remember?"

The chord progression continues, with the musician playing a melody over it that suggests the song "Will the circle be unbroken ..."

The Acknowledgment

The fourth stage of a scene is the brief but important moment of the acknowledgment. The story has been told and the action ended. Still in their positions on stage but free of their roles, the actors turn and look at Leon. Their gesture says: "We heard your story and we have done our best to fulfill it. Please accept our gift to you." It's an expression of humility, respect, and the courage to own their enactment, imperfect though it may be.

Bringing it back to the teller

In the fifth and final stage, the focus is back on the teller and the conductor. Leon nods. The conductor gives him a chance to comment.

"Did that feel like your story, Leon?"

Leon smiles at his wife in the second row. "That's our boy!" More somberly, he says, "Yeah. Being a father is complicated! My dad didn't disappoint me on purpose."

"Well, thank you very much for that story," says the conductor. Leon walks back to his seat. The actors hang up the fabric they've used and put the boxes back in position.

The conductor is speaking to the audience again. "We'd like to invite another story now, perhaps about parents and children, perhaps about something quite different. We won't forget Leon's story. But we're ready for the next one."

Corrections and Transformations

When Leon's story was over, the conductor made sure that the teller had a chance to have the last word. Enactments are never perfect. But if Leon had indicated that something about it was seriously inaccurate or missing, diminishing the scene's effectiveness for him, the conductor might have asked the actors to do a correction—a redoing of the scene incorporating Leon's comment. But Leon's response made it clear that he felt satisfied, that this scene did indeed match with his experience. In fact it's rare, with performers who know how to listen well, for tellers to need a correction.

Occasionally, after the enactment of a story that depicts a particularly unjust or unresolved experience, the conductor might invite the teller to imagine a different outcome. Then the actors play it back. This is called a transformation.

Although there are times when a transformation can be

powerfully redemptive—for the audience and the actors as well as for the teller—we've learned over time that often a story with a painful or unresolved ending will find its healing fulfillment in another teller's story. One story answers another in a subtle process of dialogue. It's not deliberate on the part of the tellers. Spontaneously, a death story early in the performance may be indirectly answered by the story of a joyous birth later on, or a story about humiliation may eventually be followed by one of triumph. We've come to invite transformations much more seldom, trusting in this tendency of the larger story to weave itself into a pattern of wholeness.

Pairs

The actors stand two-by-two across the stage. Each pair stands close together with one in front, one behind, all facing the audience. The conductor asks people to think of times when they've been aware of two contrasting or conflicting emotions going on at the same time.

"Love and disgust," calls out someone.

"OK, such as when?" asks the conductor.

"With my little 1st graders. I love them but it sometimes turns my stomach dealing with all their snot and head lice and the way some of them smell."

One pair begins. The actor in front portrays one of the teller's feelings, using sound, movement, and words. As soon as she knows which feeling her partner has chosen, the actor behind acts out the other feeling. The actors intertwine and struggle with each other, their words and non-verbal sounds in an overlapping counterpoint. Their closeness creates the illusion that this is not two actors but one person with two divergent selves.

The first pair lasts less than a minute, immediately

followed by the second. Each pair is different. The actors have tuned into different aspects of the teller's experience. One pair might happen to match the teller's experience more closely than the others, but the richness of more than one interpretation gives others in the audience a chance to see themselves in the pairs as well.

The conductor asks for more. Lots of people have their hands up. The experience of being pulled between different feelings is familiar to just about everyone, and it can be satisfying to see this inner conflict externalized.

You can use pairs in the warm-up section of a show if an audience member speaks about conflicting feelings. Pairs can also provide a change of pace after enacting two or three stories—and an opportunity to reflect on themes that have emerged. The conductor could, for example, invite the audience to think about two feelings in relation to parenting, as in Leon's story.

As well as these three basic forms—scenes, fluid sculptures, and pairs—there are many variations that might be used in a performance. We'll choose a few of these to look at.

Chorus

The actors, usually at least three, stand closely together in a clump. One begins an action, using movement and sounds or words. Instantly, the others echo this offer so that the whole chorus explores it together. Then someone else initiates a new idea, immediately adopted and amplified by everyone else. The clump may end up moving around the stage like an amoeba.

A whole story can be told in this impressionistic and non-linear way, perhaps with actors detaching themselves from the group from time to time to take on a role, then merging with the group again. Or the chorus can be a dramatic mood element in a conventional scene. Chorus was first developed by Playback performers in Australia and New Zealand.

Playback Puppets

A teller comes to the teller's chair for the next story. But the actors have disappeared behind a free-standing curtain onstage. The teller is a bit puzzled. The conductor begins the interview in the usual way. The teller launches into the story. "Pick something to be you," says the conductor, gesturing toward the curtain, above which four or five strange objects are now slowly rising. There is a purple duster, a toy broom, a laundry detergent bottle, a bald rag doll, a toilet brush. The teller gasps in surprise and the audience laughs. Then she looks more carefully. "The duster," she says. The objects sink out of sight again, the duster remaining visible a moment longer. The interview continues. The teller picks the snorkel to be the software company she's negotiating with, and the rag doll to be its annoyingly sexist logo. "Let's watch!" says the conductor. There is a moment or two of music. Then the puppets act out the story.

Amazingly, it's not hard to feel engaged, even moved by an interaction between a feather duster and a snorkel. In this imaginative, ritual context, we can readily endow household objects with human characteristics, just as small children do in their play. In a Playback performance, a scene done with "puppets" instead of visible actors can provide theatrical variety. It is an opportunity for a different kind of expression and response. Anything can serve as a puppet. Instead of coming prepared with objects, you can involve the audience in finding objects around the room—a plant, a shoe, a ruler.

Tableau Stories

Another way to render a story was developed by the Melbourne Playback Theatre company. Early in the show, as the audience is still warming up, someone might be invited to tell a story—just a little more expansive than a fluid sculpture response—from his or her place in the audience. The conductor listens, then retells the essence of the story in a series of titles: "Vanessa is late for work." "She drives very fast and almost has an accident." "When she arrives the parking lot is empty." "Then she remembers that there's no school today." After each one of these, the actors create a tableau, a sculpture that is still, not fluid, expressing one stage of the story—rather like a series of stills from a silent movie, with subtitles spoken by the conductor. And like a silent movie, there's music to help evoke the right atmosphere.

Three-sentence story

Three-sentence story was devised by Eugene Playback Theatre. The conductor invites audience members to tell a story in three sentences, condensing or rephrasing if necessary. Audiences usually enjoy this creative challenge.

A woman raises her hand. "My ten-year-old daughter was terribly worried about a school test that was coming up. I did everything I could to help her be ready. On the day of the test there was a snowstorm and school was cancelled."

Three actors stand facing the audience. After hearing all three sentences, the actor on stage right steps into the space. She takes on the role of the daughter, using voice and movement to express the essence of the girl's anxiety. Then she freezes.

The second actor steps forward. In a moment it's clear that he's portraying the mother. He puts his arms around the daughter, who can't respond because she's now a statue. His movement and words convey the mother's concern. Then he freezes too, reaching toward the daughter from across the stage.

The third actor takes a piece of white fabric and becomes a benign, mischievous snowstorm who saves the girl and her mother from the looming test. "Who needs all those standardized tests anyway?" she says, expanding the frame of the story.

All three actors freeze in an expressive configuration. The music, which has changed with each new actor, now pauses.

Three-part story

Three-part story, subsequently developed by several groups, is structurally like three-sentence, but instead of asking the teller to give three sentences, the actors themselves distill three key elements from a story told by an audience member. The three segments, each about a minute, are not necessarily chronological and not literal. The discipline is for each actor to embody and express just one key element. The third actor has less choice than the others: he will have to choose the most important character or element that has not yet been represented.

In both three-sentence and three-part story, actors use body, movement, fabric, space, voice, or words to express their part of the story. Actors can play any character or element, as long as at least one plays the teller.

Narrative V

This short form, developed by Hudson River Playback Theatre, has been widely adopted because it's effective and relatively easy to do. Actors stand in a narrow V formation (not necessarily symmetrical). The actor in front narrates the teller's short story in the third person, using gestures and language like a storyteller but not actually enacting the story. To maintain the difference between storytelling and acting, it's helpful to use the upper body rather than the whole body. Using peripheral vision, the other actors echo the narrator's gestures without looking at her. They may occasionally echo sounds as well.

Using the forms[3]

By now there are dozens of different Playback Theatre forms, developed and used by companies all over the world. No one knows them all! Some are exciting but short-lived; others prove themselves over time and are adopted by other groups, inevitably evolving further. I've listed a few of the most established and useful forms—but this is an ongoing story.

How to use them? This is a topic for a workshop, not a book. But some thoughts: first of all, although the different forms create artistic variety, the main point of having them is not to show off your skill—*it's to match the Playback response more precisely to the teller's story.* We never know what an audience member is going to say. With a repertoire of four or five short forms (and you don't need more), you can decide which one will best serve the events and meanings of what the teller has said. Sometimes it's the conductor who chooses a form, letting the performers know in a quiet aside (since the audience does not need to hear our technical terms). Or the actors themselves decide.

It's useful to think of short forms as being either narra-

---

[3]The short forms mentioned in this chapter are fluid sculptures, pairs, tableau, three-sentence story, three-part story, and narrative V. Long forms are scenes and Playback puppets. Chorus can be used as either a short or long form, or an element within a scene.

tive or non-narrative. A narrative short form, like tableau, three-part story, or narrative V, can briefly depict a story. Non-narrative short forms, such fluid sculptures or pairs, portray feeling states without narrative. So when an audience member responds to a warm-up question with a little story, you can choose to reflect that story in a narrative short form; or focus on the central emotion, playing it in a non-narrative form.

Short forms generally belong in the initial and essential warm-up phase of a performance, that period of twenty minutes or so at the beginning when you're building rapport with an audience and perhaps warming up to a theme. It's not time yet to bring someone to the stage, which asks much more from a teller than speaking from her or his relatively safe seat in the audience. Even if an eager audience member is ready to jump up onstage, it's too soon until you have heard from a number of voices, building the temporary community of this event.

When that moment comes—when you sense that the audience is at ease and ready for more—you invite them to think about a longer story, to be told from the teller's chair onstage. And at this point the implied contract with the teller changes. We're asking them to offer more, to be seen and heard by everyone, to take more of a risk. In return, they expect and deserve to see their story played out at more length. It's not fair to revert to a short form after a teller has spent six or seven minutes telling a story.

You might use short forms again if the moment calls for it, for example to reflect on a story that has been especially intense for everyone before moving on to another teller. Or to build a closure at the end of a show.

Fluid sculptures

One actor steps forward and begins a repeated sound and movement.

The other actors join in.

Actors hold a final moment.

Pairs

The pair on the left enacts an audience member's conflicting feelings about starting university.

The first pair freezes while the second pair offers their version.

Narrative V

Actors stand in a narrow V-formation.

The actor in front narrates the story, using gestures that are echoed by the others.

Story (scene)

A teller comes to the teller's chair. In conversation with the conductor, she tells a story about her little girl and her own childhood. Actors stand when they are chosen by the teller.

Teller and conductor watch as the enactment begins.

The musician improvises along with the actors.

The scene develops…

…and comes to an end.

Actors acknowledge the teller. The conductor invites the teller to comment.

Playback puppets

A duster, a snorkel, and a rag doll act out another story.

Photos of Hudson River Playback Theatre by Marjorie Berman.

4

Being a Playback Actor

Imagine you're a Playback actor, about to turn someone's life into theatre. The teller has just told a story about a tragicomic crisis at a family Thanksgiving dinner. She has picked you to play her mother. You're standing there on the stage, listening to the teller, watching her, straining to catch every nuance, trying to remember exactly who has been chosen to be the hippie uncle, wondering what on earth you're going to do to approximate running down three flights of stairs. Then the conductor says "Watch!" and you have to jump in and hope for the best. And somehow, once again, it works. Ideas come to you from who knows where; your fellow actors seem to be on the same wavelength; together, with the help of the music, you build a theatre piece with form, and meaning; and then it's over, and the teller is nodding and sighing.

Ready for Any Role

I've seen Playback actors portraying a toilet brush, an electively-mute child, an undisciplined Great Dane, a newborn baby, a coffee table, a stranger who dies in a post office, a beloved car, a wounded bird of prey. Some roles are challenging artistically—how would *you* play a coffee table?—and some emotionally. Playback actors have to be prepared for anything.

Choosing an actor to be a character in a story is an intuitive process. Holding the image of his friend or himself or whoever it is in his mind, the teller looks at the actors and senses which one best fits his inward picture. The match may well not follow appearance, age, or gender. Women are often picked to play men and vice versa. The actor needs to be able to enter the role free of stereotypes or self-consciousness, not always an easy task. Tellers sometimes make telepathic choices when they cast their stories, picking an actor for a role which, unknown to the teller, is in fact part of the actor's real life. This can be helpful, such as the time a teller chose an actor who is the head nurse in a hospital neo-natal unit to play the midwife in a childbirth scene.

But sometimes there may be painful parallels between the role and your own personal life. I remember a scene in which an audience actor courageously fulfilled the role of a mother whose son was killed in a motorcycle accident, only later revealing that she herself had lost a son in the same way. A woman whose childhood was dominated by a violent father was asked to portray an abused child. An actor living with AIDS was chosen to play someone who died of AIDS.

Is this asking too much of Playback actors? After all, it is important that the work is beneficial for those who perform it, as well as for those to whom it is offered. This is not a theatre where the actors' wellbeing is to be sacrificed to the success of the performance.

A Playback actor always has the option to say "No, I'm sorry, I just can't play that role." I've seen it happen a few times, and I remember one time, many years ago, when I needed to say that myself. Mourning a friend's suicide, I was asked to play a woman who had killed herself in the same shocking way. That was very early in our Playback explorations. I've never needed to refuse a role again, though like all actors I've occasionally been asked to play some very difficult ones. What changed for me, and I think this happens to most people who practice Playback for a while, was that through the work itself my personal resources grew, enabling me to find the strength and empathy to approach any role without danger to myself.

On the other hand, roles can be hard just because they are so far from the actor's experience or personality. A shy man may have difficulty being sexy when a role calls for it. An art teacher may have to work hard to be convincing as a brisk CEO.

Perhaps the most demanding role of all is one that traditional actors are not usually called upon to master—being oneself. Playback actors begin and end the show as themselves. In between scenes, there they are on the stage, just Andy and Nora and Lee. It's not so easy to be fully yourself on a stage, especially when you have to remain in that delicately balanced state of receptivity and poised spontaneity. You don't know what the stories will be; you may be picked for a role where you can spread your acting wings, or for a role that you will find painful, or disappointingly slight, or you may not be picked at all. No matter what happens, the scene will be over in five or ten minutes, and you will have to let go of whatever has been stirred up in you and be open to the next story.

So Playback actors need a great deal of emotional and expressive flexibility, grounded in self-awareness. No one is ever free from the features of their personality or from life problems. But actors who know themselves well can find resources to fulfill any role. They can go deeply into a character, summoning all the intensity called for by the story, and then step out of it when the scene is over. They develop strength and agility like a gymnast, using emotion and expressiveness rather than muscles.

How do they do it? First of all, it's my observation that Playback tends to attract unusually mature and generous people as performers. Jonathan Fox talks about the strength of the "citizen actor," who studies and performs Playback Theatre as an avocation not a career, whose acting is enriched by the experiences of an ordinary life. Secondly, Playback groups, when they are starting out or looking for new members, place emotional maturity and self-awareness high on the list of qualities that they are seeking. And thirdly, the work itself promotes growth in this direction. You can't spend years listening to stories and telling your own in Playback's kindly atmosphere without growing in self-knowledge, tolerance, and love.

Expressiveness and Spontaneity

Not only do the actors have to be open to any role, they also need to be fully expressive in that role. They must *be* the character or element in the scene, and find actions, words, movements, sounds that will bring it to life as vividly as possible. To people beginning in the work, the task can seem complex and daunting. I've found that new Playback actors are often cautious about using their voices and bodies. They tend to fall back on stereotyped representations. They say they just don't know how to be a sadistic hairdresser, or a disease.

But they learn. Any training in Playback acting, whether in a one-day workshop or in the months after joining a company, gives new actors a chance to explore their spontaneity in an accepting and supportive environment. Every rehearsal or workshop includes games and warm-ups that invite you to try new dimensions of expression. And as you discover a greater and greater expressiveness, you bring it to the roles that you are chosen for in the scenes.

One warm-up is called "Sound and Movement."[1] We're all standing in a circle. "OK," says the leader, "one

---

[1] This exercise—and a number of other Playback practices—was inspired by the work of Joseph Chaikin of the Open Theatre, although his "Sound and movement" exercise was actually closer to the more advanced version described below. *References and Resources* lists several sources for theatre games.

at a time, everyone's going to make a sound and some kind of movement to go with it. It can be anything, but make it short. Then we'll all echo it together." One person starts. She undulates her arms around her body, her voice whooping like a siren. There's a beat after she finishes; then, in unison, everyone copies her sound and movement. The next person in the circle is new to this. He pauses, embarrassed. "I can't think of anything," he says. "Don't think!" says the leader. "Let your body just do something!" He pauses again, then flaps his arms like a bird, making little chirruping noises. It's very simple and small, but that's OK. We all follow. In coming weeks he will find himself making sounds and movements that he never imagined could be part of his repertoire. His freedom and playfulness will grow, his cautiousness diminish.

There are countless activities that Playback groups use to develop the actors' expressiveness—countless because in the nature of this spontaneous work, new ideas are born at almost every rehearsal. It is enormously satisfying to stretch yourself in this way; to push back the boundaries of what is possible for you in your movements, interactions, sounds; to let the fear of looking ridiculous fall away, replaced by a delight in your own and others' inventiveness. Keith Johnstone says in his book *Impro*: "It's the most marvelous thing about improvisation: you are suddenly in contact with people who are unbounded, whose imagination seems to function without limit."[2]

In another group, where the members have been working together for six years, they are warming up with a more advanced version of "Sound and Movement." One person steps into the middle of the circle. Following the impulses

---

[2]Keith Johnstone, *Impro: Improvisation and the Theatre*, (New York: Theatre Arts, 1979), 100.

of his body and his emotions, he moves this way and that, strange vocal sounds flying around the space. Gradually his movement acquires form and rhythm, and a building sense of anger. Howling, swinging his arms and stomping like an enraged gorilla, he makes eye contact with someone else in the circle. She mirrors his actions. They stay in this fierce dance for a minute; then, still moving, they switch places. The woman continues his movement, but then she begins to let her body move according to its own inner imperatives until the movement and sounds she is making are hers. She chooses another woman to join her. The cycle starts over again.

By the time the activity is over, several people in the group have let themselves feel and express very strong emotions. There has been sobbing, cackling, screaming. Years of trust have allowed this circle to be a safe arena for any expression. The actors have knowingly invited deep feelings to emerge by using their bodies without reserve. No-one is disconcerted by the intensity. At the end, they take deep breaths, relax, throw an arm around a shoulder here and there, and they're ready to move on.

Forbidden Zones

One thing that always happens in the process—and it's one of the reasons why some people prefer not to venture into this realm—is that the zone of acceptable actions begins to include some that in other contexts would seem rather rude or crazy. When you take down the barriers to playfulness and spontaneity, you also let in dark and unruly energies that most of us try hard to keep hidden from others and even ourselves. In the privacy of the rehearsal space you may find yourself doing and saying things that would disturb the neighbors and your Aunt Pauline.

50

There is a tie-in with trust and group-building. People are not going to risk their public image until they feel safe with one another. In the original company, it took us several years to approach this stage. Once we did, the sphere of our group creativity expanded enormously, as did the personal expressiveness that each of us felt. Some of us came to depend on this regular opportunity to exercise ourselves in the further reaches of playful absurdity and grotesqueness. It was a healing antidote to the other craziness of the "real" world.

We are all fairly ordinary responsible people, and fully capable of behaving with conventional restraint when we need to. This licentiousness has never been apparent in performances. The fact is that such a degree of freedom in rehearsal times leads to the freedom to be available and expressive to our fullest capacity as we act out audience members' stories.

The Actor's Sense of Story

As we saw in chapter 2, the effectiveness of a Playback scene depends a great deal on the actors' sense of story, that aesthetic feel for form and the archetypal story shape. And this aesthetic sense must be in service to an empathic, almost intuitive understanding of the essence of the teller's experience. Both elements are crucial to the success of a Playback scene.

At a Playback training workshop, a woman tells a story about a child she has recently worked with in a psychiatric hospital.

"This story's about Sam, who's eleven. He'd been doing pretty well in treatment, and they decided to discharge him. The problem is they sent him home to his mother. She's terminally ill and really not able to supervise him properly. They live in

a very poor neighborhood in the city—there's lots of drugs and violence. I was afraid for him and so were several other people at the hospital, but there was nothing we could do, once it was decided that he should go home. That was about three weeks ago." The teller pauses, covering her face with her hands. "And then just the other day we heard that he'd been attacked by some older kids who had fireworks for the Fourth of July. They set off a firecracker in his face. Sam was hurt very badly. They say his eyesight is permanently damaged and his face is all scarred. I feel so helpless—whatever we were able to do for him meant nothing once he was out of our care."

In the enactment, most of the actors were united in their perception of the core of this experience. They built their story around the teller's sorrow at her inability to save Sam from his fate. But an actor playing one of the bullying teenagers was working from a different agenda. Playing his relatively minor role very forcefully, he initiated an interaction with the actor playing Sam in which the issue became a kind of delinquent peer pressure on Sam to disobey his mother. His reading of the meaning of the story derailed the scene from the aesthetic integrity it had built up to that point. And it undercut the enactment's impact for the teller—she no longer recognized it as her story.

This was a moment when a failure to grasp the meaning of the teller's experience spoiled the effectiveness of the enactment. It's always possible to seriously misread the essence of the story, although it happens far less often than you might think. When it does, there is usually some reason for it, something that is blocking the actor's sensitivity. In this case, the actor in question was someone who by his own self-description loved to be at the center of the action and tended to have difficulty with minor roles. Helping actors find the flexibility and humility they need for Playback work is a task that companies sometimes have to deal with.

Sometimes the actors may be on target with their feeling for the story's essence, but fall short of creating a story shape to embody it. (Music can be an extremely helpful ally in this respect—see chapter 6.) Often the story contour is weakest at the beginning or the end. In their anxiety to reach the climactic event, actors sometimes skip over the essential stage of setting the scene for what is to follow. In a story about a frightening encounter on a dark street, the actors hastened to the confrontation itself, which was much less dramatic than if they had first of all established the contrasting safety of the teller's home. Endings can be hard, too. You need courage to know that the last word has been spoken, the story has been told, anything further will weaken it.

It takes practice to master these aspects of the Playback work. But as they tell and enact story after story, actors develop the twin abilities to listen with empathy and to create coherent shapes from raw-edged chunks of life. In the mix of rewards and motivations that draw them onward, art, exhilaration, and the delight of giving all play a part.

Once I saw a relatively inexperienced Playback team break through to a new level of mastery, and it was generosity that led them there. At a rehearsal, Tim seemed troubled and sad. Invited to tell his story if he wished, he said that it was the first anniversary of his sister's violent death. He told us about his struggle between everyday obligations and the desire to withdraw into his lonely grief. In their loving concern for him, the actors rendered his story with a degree of aesthetic grace, authenticity, and economy that they had never before achieved. At the end, the teller's actor pushed herself free of the actor who was embodying Tim's feeling of terrible loss. She gazed out into that private space of theatrical soliloquy with tears in her eyes. "I wonder if I'm going to be able to keep going." No one tried to answer. No one tried to soothe away Tim's grief. The actors let this last line simply express the anguish, unresolved as it was.

Teamwork

Many of the factors we've looked at so far in this chapter played a part in the success of this scene. The actors' expressiveness and spontaneity enabled them to fully embody the roles they were chosen for, even though some were not easy. They clearly sensed the meaning of Tim's experience, and were able to express it in the form of a story. And there was another important factor present too—the team's ability to work co-creatively with each other.

Part of the task of improvising is having the guts to act on your own impulses and inspirations even when you might be tempted to ignore or censor them. But you also have to be responsive to the impulses and inspirations of everyone else. Keith Johnstone describes this dialectic in terms of offers which are either accepted or blocked. When you don't have the black-and-white clarity of a script behind you, the scene can only proceed by a series of offers. In Playback, unlike some other forms of improvisation, we do at least know the rough outline of the story. Still, we don't know exactly how it is going to go until it is happening. In the scene just mentioned, one actor, Dennis, began the action by making a telephone call to Angela, the teller's actor: "Brrring! Brrring!" Whatever thoughts any of the other actors may have had about how the scene might start, they had to go with Dennis's offer of the phone call. If Angela had ignored it in order to begin her own way, she would have been blocking the offer, and the result would have been not only confusion but a sense of stalled energy.

Every onward step in the scene is an offer of some kind. And every offer is a test of the actors' readiness to initiate and receive. Often the hardest offer to accept is the exit line, which usually needs to be spoken by the teller's actor. Can you, in your supporting role, let this be the last word? Can you open your ears to the subtle cadence of the ending? Once you get used to listening for it, this moment becomes almost unmistakable.

Voice and Language

The basic tools of the traditional actor—use of the voice, the body, the space—are also important in Playback Theatre. For Playback actors, most of whom do not come from theatre backgrounds, learning to use the voice usually has more to do with acquiring boldness than technique. The ambivalence of an inexperienced actor often shows itself in an almost inaudible voice—"I'm here on stage but please don't notice me."

One exercise that helps people overcome this kind of shyness begins with everyone toe-to-toe in two lines. Each set of partners is asked to invent a two-line dialogue. There's no need to be profound or even to make sense. Then, simultaneously, we all say our lines to each other, very quietly. We take a step back, and the dialogues are repeated, now a little louder. The process continues until there are two lines of people at the extremities of the space, shouting their lines at the tops of their voices so as to be heard over the cacophony. By now, everyone is not only yelling but gesticulating wildly, their whole bodies involved in the effort to communicate. Then the leader asks each pair to shout out its dialogue, one at a time. The actors are still carried by the momentum of the group crescendo, their self-consciousness gone, at least temporarily. "Tell your dog to leave me alone!" bawls out the first one. "I burnt the potatoes!" screams his partner. And so on.

Once people have got beyond the initial fear of being heard, they are ready to work on projecting their voices and pacing their speech so that it can be clearly understood by everyone in the audience. One of the reasons that these tasks can be especially challenging in Playback Theatre is, of course, that it's hard to speak with assurance when the words you are saying are your own, invented on the spot, not the carefully crafted words of a master playwright. What if they sound stupid? Or what if one of your fellow actors starts to speak at the same time? Like every other artistic issue in Playback Theatre, the question of voice and language turns out to be also a question of intuitiveness and group trust.

And the aesthetic challenge is there, too. Playback actors are called upon to be artists with language, to create the dialogue that will tell the story, and to do so with as much sensitivity, aesthetic awareness, and economy as they can. Language seldom has to stand by itself and sometimes can be dispensed with altogether if a scene is enacted just in mime or movement. But in most situations the words spoken will be a focal part of the enactment. The language may be casual and naturalistic, or heightened like poetry. In fluid sculptures and pairs, too, sparse and carefully chosen words can be an artistic complement to the action, like an elliptical, evocative line of words on a painting.

In our company we've had two or three people who had a gift for language, who somehow could always find words that were precise and fresh and rich. Others were at their strongest with movement, or imaginative staging. Although it's important for everyone to have all these skills in some measure, it is an overall strength for a company if there is scope for each member to use her or his special gifts.

The Body

The actors' physicality is another important aspect. Playback rehearsals, workshops, and warm-ups before

56

performances almost always begin with vigorous physical activity to wake up the body's strength, its emotions, its expressiveness. We also work on accessing the huge variety of posture and gesture that is available to us in our task of assuming different roles. We discover that characters can suggest themselves through the body and the voice as well as the other way around. If you take an unfamiliar posture—say, inflating your chest and sticking it out—and walk around like that, letting the rest of your body align itself as it wants to, you will probably find that you begin to feel like someone who moves like this, whose voice and thoughts may be quite different from your own. Depending on the whole pattern of your body, and your own kinesthetic associations, you could find yourself feeling like a muscle-bound truck driver, or a big-busted flirt, or a shy five-year-old.

Being comfortable with one's body as a Playback actor includes being ready to touch and be touched. In fluid sculptures and pairs, where the aesthetic success depends on the visible, organic connection between the actors, dynamic physical contact is very important. In a fluid sculpture, Ginny expresses a teller's feeling of being burdened by draping herself over Nick's body. Along with the experience that they are depicting, there is also the reality that this man and woman are in intimate contact. They are sensually aware of the features of each other's body, its weight and shape. They need to be comfortable with this, to be able to manage whatever feelings might be stirred up by such intimacy. Scenes, too, often require the actors to interact physically, as well as in movement and dialogue—sometimes forcefully, sometimes tenderly. Fights and lovemaking and cuddling children and dancing are part of living. We have to be ready to play back such moments when they come up in a story.

Again, the ability to work in close physical contact is also a function of group process. It's a sign of a certain level of trust when the actors find themselves able to interact with one another's bodies in the interests of expressiveness.

The Space and the Props

The actors' arena is the stage. In Playback Theatre this is often not an actual stage at all, but simply a cleared space in the front of a room. We must find a way to transform it into that magical zone in which anything can happen. The visual set-up helps—the colorful prop tree, the chairs and boxes and instruments surrounding an invitingly empty space. (See chapter 7.) It's important for the actors to be aware of basic stagecraft, to know how the impact of your action will be affected by how you use the space. The conductor may do some rudimentary blocking as part of the interview—"OK, we'll have the circus ring over there," pointing to the far side of the stage, "and the ambulance here," indicating the area downstage and closer to the teller. But it is mostly up to the actors to improvise the layout of the space, using the boxes and cloth props, and then to choreograph their own interactions inside this elementary stage set. Unlike regular theatre, the placement of the action has to take two sets of sightlines into consideration, the teller's as well as the audience's. For this reason, many scenes will begin upstage left, progressively approaching the teller so that the climax and conclusion take place downstage right.

The props themselves, as we've seen, are no more than a set of boxes—either the traditional plastic milk crates or specially-made wooden boxes—and a collection of lengths of fabric, chosen for their colors and textures. Some of the fabric pieces might have a neck hole or eye holes. There might be one with loops for hands to go through in the corners, so that an actor could use it as wings. But we've found through experimentation that the less structured the cloth props are, the more expressive and versatile they can be. With the audience's imagination already engaged, a piece of fabric can be a convincing bride's dress or animal skin. And it is perfectly possibly for the boxes to be believable as television sets or birthday cakes or sand castles.

Usually, the fabric pieces are most useful as suggestive mood elements rather than as costumes. One of the mistakes that new actors are likely to make is to over-use the cloth, swathing themselves in pieces of fabric no matter what their roles. It does not add anything when an actor, picked to be a mother, ties a piece of fabric around his waist to represent an apron or a vestigial skirt! Often, the impulse to do this has a lot to do with the new actor's insecurity—taking time at the prop tree during the setting-up is a way to postpone the moment of launching the scene, and any costume feels safer than none. More experienced actors use the fabric props very sparsely, usually for mood or to concretize an element in the story. A long piece of black cloth twisted between two actors might depict a destructive family bond. An actor playing a character who is cut off from other people might cover her head with gauzy layers of cloth and shed them one by one as she learns to reach out.[3] The boxes, too, lend themselves to non-literal uses—a pedestal for an arrogant doctor, a cage for a frightened child.

Art and Style: Some Considerations

A ten-year-old girl tells about running away from home when she was eight. We see the teller's actor and her friend playing in the woods, finding an old shed and trying to set fire to it, convincing the owner that they're innocent when

---

[3]Some groups feel that their enactments are more cluttered than enriched by the use of cloth props and have dispensed with them altogetther.

*he surprises them. At the same time, on the other side of the
stage, the girl's mother is wondering where her daughter is.
She peers out the window, calls her name from the front door.
Getting more and more upset, she calls the police and alerts
them to the child's absence. These two scenes play side-by-side
in counterpoint, until the children are found by the police and
brought home to an angry but relieved mother, and the two
scenes become one.*

This scene made use of a technique we call *Focus*. The
actors modulated their action and dialogue so that the audience's attention was drawn back and forth from one mini-
scene to the other. Both the teller's actor and the mother were
speaking their thoughts aloud, as well as talking to the other
characters. But each set of actors would pause regularly to
allow space for the others. The effect was a bit like using a
spotlight or a movie camera to shift the attention from one
part of the action to another.

Many scenes include action going on simultaneously in
more than one location. Being able to manoeuver the focus
in this way can help a lot in making them dramatic.

The Playback team has a choice about where to place
the enactment on the spectrum from realism to abstraction. This theatre is always about the subjective reality of
the teller's experience, and there's room for a great deal of
liberty to be taken with the external details. Features of the
original experience can be telescoped or exaggerated according
to the story's meaning (for example the prolongation of the
climactic naked confrontation in Elaine's story in chapter
2.) Or an event can be translated into another medium. At a
conference of music therapists, the actors had to enact a story
about a music therapy session. Rather than try to recreate
the therapy itself, which would have been very hard to do
convincingly in front of an audience of experts, the actors

used dance as a metaphor to convey the co-creative interaction of therapist and client.

There can be a danger in going too far in the direction of abstract representation. Above all we need to see a story. If the actors launch themselves into the stratosphere of symbolic action, the essential particularity of the teller's story can get lost. The meaning of the experience can only express itself in the actual events of the story, where it happened, when, who was there, what did they do and say.

It's often a combination of the literal and the abstract that most strongly carries the story. Sometimes, as we've seen, actors are chosen to play inanimate or non-physical aspects of the experience. A technique based on the idea of the Greek chorus, the *mood sculpture*,[4] uses two or three actors working closely together to express in sound and movement some important dynamic or presence, either amplifying the main action or in contrast to it. Standing side-by-side, taking visual and sound cues from the person in the center of the mood sculpture, they act as one entity. As with pairs, the audience accepts the illusion that the mood sculpture is somehow part of the teller. In a scene about a student's secret romantic fascination with a beautiful girl in his physics class, three actors position themselves behind the teller's actor. He pretends to be very cool, barely aware of the girl. "Oh, hi. Sorry, I didn't catch your name." Behind him, the mood sculpture writhes in torments of teenage lust.

How Far Can I Go?

It's hard for an actor to resist the temptation to ask questions during the interview. You almost always feel

---

[4]This was originally called a lineal. In its more developed form, the mood sculpture is a chorus—see page 40.

that you don't have enough information. But you keep your silence, because you know how undramatic it would be to break into the delicate web of anticipation that is being woven. And you have also learned that really there's no such thing as enough information; in the end you are always thrown onto your empathy, your intuition, and your creativity.

When you don't know all the details, you have to make them up. Actors are often fearful that they will say or do the wrong thing, that they will offend the teller or be embarrassingly far off the mark. But even with new actors, these things seldom happen. Why not? Because the actors' basic generosity allows them to access their intuition, and most of the time the imaginative leaps they make are true to the teller's experience, either in spirit or literally, even when this particular detail may not have emerged in the interview. Often at the end of a scene, the teller says something like "How did they know that my teacher talked about the Second World War all the time?" Or "You know, it *was* cucumbers that we were planting. I'd forgotten that."

On those occasions when a detail is wrong enough to matter to the teller, he always has a chance to say so at the end of the scene. But he is unlikely to be hurt or offended, because the intention of the actors is clearly to serve his story rather than their egos or the audience's desire for entertainment. Usually the teller is satisfied just to have had a chance to comment, but once in a while the conductor may ask the actors to redo the scene incorporating the correction.

Making creative guesses to flesh out the scene is not the same as interpreting or analyzing the teller's story, though the line between the two can be delicate. Playback Theatre concerns itself with the great richness of the story; the actual events and the teller's subjective experience of them. It is usually misplaced for the conductor or the actors to make explicit what they think are underlying psychological impli-cations. If they fully honor the story as it is told, there will be wisdom in their enactment, and if the teller is ready, he or she will receive it.

The Actor's Rewards

For most Playback actors, this work is neither glamorous nor remunerative. So what keeps them involved, often for years? As I mentioned earlier, Playback Theatre is an inher-ently nurturing environment for all concerned. The training and rehearsal process leads to personal growth as people develop expressiveness and self-awareness—and as they tell their own stories, the old stories and the new, the deep, painful stories, the silly ones and the triumphant ones. The limitations of personality are softened or even transcended as the actors try out new ways of being through their roles in other people's stories. It can feel wonderful to access a wholly unsuspected part of oneself—to shine in the role of the swaggering star of the ski slopes when in real life you keep your sexuality under wraps.

You learn skills that you can use in a variety of other contexts. Playback actors who also perform in the traditional theatre bring a deepened humanity to their roles. Therapists and teachers acquire perspectives and techniques directly relevant to their work. Writers and artists hone their aesthetic sense and gather rich material. And everyone can apply the lessons of give-and-take, offering and not blocking, to the improvisational art of communication.

There is also, for the actors, the unique satisfaction of knowing that you have brought someone's story to life; knowing that your creativity has been the gem-cutter that has released the subtle beauty of the teller's story. And you have done this together. You are part of a team. The challenges you share, the chartless territory you explore together bonds you like comrades-in-arms. Unlike soldiers, though, your work is not the destruction of life, but the celebration of it.

5

Conducting

In the first few years of the original company, Jonathan was always the conductor. Sometime after we had established our "First Friday " series, he had to be away one evening. No problem; we decided that one of the actors would conduct the show. It was a fiasco. I remember watching in dismay from the musician's chair, trying to do what I could to help, but seeing the actors, tellers, audience, and most of all the unfortunate conductor himself sink into a morass. That's how we learned that you need thorough preparation to step into this role. What came naturally to Jonathan was for most other people, including those of us who had seen him time after time, a very specialized and sophisticated set of tasks.

The double metaphor of the name "conductor" points to two aspects of the conductor's job. It refers to the role of the orchestral conductor—directing a group of performers so they can work together and so the pieces they collectively create are organized and beautiful—and also to the conduction of energy between all those present. The conductor is the conduit, the channel through which audience and actors can meet. There is a third aspect of the conductor's job: building the series of intimate though ephemeral relationships with the tellers.

These three areas of focus—the story, the audience, and the teller—each call for a different set of tasks and roles. As the conductor, you must be able to move smoothly between all of them, often managing several at a time. You will probably need to be, at different moments, a master of ceremonies, a director, a therapist, a performer, a showman, a shaman, a clown, a diplomat. Hardly anyone is naturally good at all of the conductor's roles. You have to consciously develop yourself in the areas that may not be your personal strong points. A dazzling showman may need to practice therapist-like listening skills. Someone who can craft a story with a poet's precision may need to work on being a diplomatic liaison person.

With hindsight, it's not surprising that my poor friend came a cropper. But it certainly is possible to grow into the conductor role with training and practice.

The Conductor as Master of Ceremonies: Attending to the Audience

As the conductor, you hold the whole event in a meta-phorical embrace, gentle and steady. You are the representative, the front person, for the performing team. It is up to you to see that the audience feels at ease, that essential standards of respect and safety are upheld, that newcomers understand what Playback Theatre is and what may be expected of them. You need to feel comfortable with being in a position of focus and with being the pivot on which the whole performance will turn. As a performer you must be both authoritative and entertaining. There may be hard decisions to be made. Which teller are you going to choose when several are offering their stories? If the first two tellers are men, do you make an effort to find a woman to tell the third story? Are there subgroups in the audience which need to be acknowledged? Should you go with a request for "one more story" when your own sense of time and drama tell you that it's time to end?

These are all aspects of the conductor's task of attending to the audience. When you are running a Playback event that is not a performance, for example a workshop or a training group, the issues remain more or less the same. You still need to attend to the larger group.

I'm directing a short performance as part of a conference presentation for professionals in the field of therapeutic recreation. (We'll come back to this show three times during this chapter, to look at the conductor's process in the three areas of focus I mentioned above.) The audience is small, about fifteen people, none of whom have ever seen Playback Theatre before. To help everyone warm up, including ourselves, we invite the audience to join us in a circle in the "stage" area—really just the space in front of the room. I'm glad to see that they are mostly wearing exercise pants or jeans, much more conducive to action than the elegant but restricting formality that you usually see at professional conferences. I feel I can ask them to move. Together we all do a round of "Sound and Movement." Some people are expansive and expressive, others shy. Everyone takes part. We each introduce ourselves, saying our names and something that we like. "Little kids," says one woman. "Chocolate!" says someone else. I notice that they seem relaxed, in good spirits. Some seem to be friends and co-workers, others have got to know each other over the four days of the conference. The woman who has been our liaison is there. She's already told me how challenging and tiring it has been to organize this conference.

They take their seats, and we begin. I tell them, briefly, what Playback Theatre is, and I outline our plan for the presentation. I tell them that for several years our group has been doing this work with disturbed children. Once they experience it for themselves, I say, they might see how it could be used with their own clients.

"This is the last day of the conference, right? How has it been for you?"

As the conductor, one of my tasks at this moment is to help them be fully here in this time and place that we are sharing, to become co-creators of whatever it is that we will build together. I know that it will help in this process to acknowledge here-and-now concerns and preoccupations. If I ask questions that they find they want to answer, that are not threatening or obscure, I will begin to communicate to them that it is safe here, we can be trusted with their stories.

Several people start to respond, including Carla, the conference organizer. It's always good to have a chance to acknowledge the people who are at the heart of an event. They're likely to be well-connected with many people there, and their active participation will encourage others.

"It's been great, but I'm *so* glad it's just about over," says Carla.

"Watch!"

The actors do a fluid sculpture that Carla nods vehemently to. Now everyone has seen the essential Playback process—that translation of experience into drama.

"How has the food been?" There are laughs and groans. (Why am I asking this particular question? Perhaps in part because food has already been mentioned in our warm-up; and I also know from experience that food is often a good topic for group building. These are hardly thoughts—just fleeting points of awareness.)

It turns out that the hotel meals have been very disappointing. The audience hoots appreciatively as the actors sag and gag on stage.

We do one or two more fluid sculptures, and then I ask for a story. I take a few minutes to warm them up to this next phase. As I talk, I'm walking back and forth across the stage area. I'm reaching out to them with my voice, my gestures, making sure to include everyone in my eye contact. I know that what I say and do in this moment can, if I do it right, help build the group's trust in me. And it can also catalyze that magical process that reaches into memory and emotion and calls forth stories.

"Anything that's happened to you can be a Playback story—something from this morning, from work, from your childhood, a dream, even something that you're thinking about that hasn't happened yet."

A woman raises her hand. "I've got a good one," she says, looking around at her friends for encouragement and getting it. But she's a bit dismayed when she realizes that she has to come to the teller's chair on stage. Her friends urge her to get up.

Her story is about a recurring nightmare. She woke up this morning in her hotel room, panicked from yet another version of the dream. In it, she realizes that her ten-year-old son is missing and she can't find him anywhere. Slightly apprehensive, like many new tellers, Carolyn has a tendency to cope by looking for laughs. The audience, sharing her nervousness, is ready to find everything funny too. But it is clearly not a funny story. I acknowledge its dimension by maintaining my own seriousness, asking questions that take the story deeper.

I want to make sure that the audience feels engaged and included. As she tells the story, I turn towards them every now and then, repeating key information, making sure that Carolyn and I don't withdraw into an exclusive little dyad. I look for ways to draw the others in. It turns out that there was a big party last night. The teller and her roommate were enjoying the festivities until three in the morning.

"Who else was celebrating last night?" I ask the audience. Wide grins as most hands go up. (Two of the actors raise their hands too. On our drive to the conference they had talked about the late-night drumming party they attended.)

This seems like a good opportunity to bring audience members into the action. I ask Carolyn to choose one of her colleagues to play the role of her roommate in the hotel. She chooses her friend Amy, who did in fact share her room. At one point in the enactment I ask the audience to play, from their seats, the role of Carolyn's neighbors who joined in the search. They're happy to do this. At the right moment, one of them helps to move the story along by saying: "Yes, I saw your son, over there."

By the end of the scene, the audience is settling in to the idea of stories. If we had more time there'd be lots more. But I'm aware that we need to move on. We end the show with some pairs. Carolyn's story has given us a strong theme.

"Who else here is a parent?" Many hands go up, actors and audience alike.

"What are two feelings that you've had as a parent, feelings that might pull you in different directions?"

We do pairs about the experience of wanting to keep one's children close, and needing to let them go. Bringing our focus back to the conference topic for the last pair, I ask for two feelings about what it's like to be a recreation worker. Everyone nods agreement as one person talks about the satisfactions of the work, on the one hand, and, on the other, the stresses on one's personal life that come from working afternoon and evening hours. There's a great deal of energy and release as they watch this one acted out.

Our show has combined performance and sharing, ritual and informality. Now, at the end, the other performers and I stand together and bow in acceptance of the audience's applause.

The Conductor Up Close: Attending to the Teller

At the same time as you are developing your connection to the whole group, and their connections to each other, you are also building a relationship, brief but significant, with the teller. You are in the paradoxical situation of establishing intimacy with one person in the midst of a public event. The delicacy of this relationship calls for a different set of skills.

"I've got a good one."

When Carolyn comes to tell her story, I am alert from the first moment to anything that can help me connect with her. We are about to enter a collaboration together. We have never met. I need to earn her trust if this is going to work. I notice that she's confident, a person who's used to attention, perhaps, but still she's nervous about taking this new risk. She doesn't seem comfortable with the physical closeness of our chairs on stage.

Most people find this a little disconcerting. They've been relating to you as a performer, getting used to you at a distance, and now here you are close enough to count each other's freckles. I try to put her at her ease by keeping my body very contained—I don't lean toward her or put my arm around the back of her chair, things I well might do with a teller whom I knew already. I match my voice and manner to her own, rather crisp and businesslike.

"This is Carolyn, right?" Thank goodness, I remember her name from our introductions earlier.

Her story is strong, with the universal theme of a mother's fear for the safety of her child. Carolyn's terror is very real, even though it's a dream. She reports later that she feels stirred up telling and watching her story, but sitting beside me she keeps her feelings all but hidden.

It's not at all unusual for a teller to be deeply moved as he watches his story. Sometimes even the telling itself is painful. The conductor needs to be prepared to offer support and comfort, to convey that tears or anger are all right here, that all of us, Playback team and audience, can be patient with a teller who needs time to find the right words for something that is struggling into the light.

Carolyn starts telling about her dream. When she pauses, I have a question. "Carolyn, hold on a moment. Can you pick one of the actors to play you in the story?"

This request immediately takes her story into the realm of co-creation with me and with the actors. From now on, as we continue the interview, she—and the audience—will be picturing the action that is going to take place in a minute or two. She gazes at the actors as she talks, seeing her son, herself, the kidnapper superimposed on them.

My interruption is also a reminder to her and to the audience that as the conductor I hold a particular responsibility. Although I am in artistic partnership with the other performers, and although we all, including the audience, will co-create this event, it is the conductor whose hands are on the steering wheel, so to speak. With a fragile or confused teller I may need to guide the telling of the story by asking frequent questions. With someone like Carolyn, apparently secure about herself and her story, my questions will be fewer. But she and the audience will sense my authority. Anyone telling a personal story in this public situation is likely to be feeling, to some degree, vulnerable and exposed. They deserve the conductor's strength.

When the conductor needs to break in to the teller's account, for the sake of clarity, economy, or collaboration, it may feel awkward. Interrupting doesn't come easily to many people learning to be in this role, especially nice, considerate people who are used to being sensitive listeners. In this context you can soften a necessary interruption with a fleeting touch on the knee or shoulder, and show by your words, your tone of voice, and use of the teller's name, that you are doing with this with respect and empathy.

The actors bring Carolyn's story to an end. The focus comes back to the teller. This is another potentially vulnerable moment. Everyone is looking at her to see how she has responded to the scene. Again, I have to find the right way to be supportive. I want her to know that I am there to help her deal with whatever her responses might be. This enactment has been powerful, and I'm aware that the nightmare was very recent. Carolyn remains quite contained. But in spite of her reserve, I can feel that she is shaken. She welcomes the invitation to come up with a new ending for the story.

What if the teller is unmoved, or clearly disappointed? It's important for us, the Playback team, to avoid the trap of needing any particular response from the teller. All we can do is our best, in our respectful way. The teller is not there to oblige us with a catharsis or expressions of admiration. Our job is to convey acceptance, no matter what the teller's reaction might be. (On extremely rare occasions we have encountered a teller who has apparently wanted only to manipulate or draw attention in a neurotic way. At such a moment, the conductor does whatever is needed to maintain the Playback group's integrity. "I'm sorry, we're not here to make fools of ourselves or of anyone else. If you'd like to tell a genuine experience, we can enact it for you; otherwise we're going to move on to another teller.")

When the scene is over the conductor asks the teller a question such as: "Did that feel like what happened?" or: "Did that capture the essence of your story?" You are not inviting a critique but encouraging the teller to attend to the parts of the enactment that especially resonated with her. You probably know already anyway: when the teller is engaged by the scene she is *literally* moved as she watches. Her breathing changes, she might lean forward in her seat, or nod, or laugh. A teller who has been completely motionless is probably just being polite if he says yes, that was just right. If he says no, the conductor may ask the actors to re-do the scene or part of it. Or it may seem sufficient for him simply to say what was missing. Occasionally a teller remains dissatisfied no matter what we do. At such times we have to live with the discomfort this creates, for ourselves and the audience as well as for the teller.

Carolyn has no corrections to suggest. But her story invites transformation. She's very absorbed as the new ending is acted out. I'm glad to see that she's more and more at ease in the teller's chair. I'm hoping that she'll feel, when it's all over, that she's glad she took the risk, that it was worth the awkwardness of revealing herself in public to see her story and to feel some movement and change in relation to it. And I want her to realize that her story has also been a gift to others. I thank her, for all of us.

Carolyn goes back to her seat, settling in with a few words to Amy. They're both audience members again.

The Conductor as Theatre Director: Attending to the Story

A person comes to the teller's chair with something in his mind, a memory, a dream, maybe a series of related events. As the conductor, your job is to find out what it is, to draw the story out from its home in the teller's memory into the public realm, and to shape it if necessary before handing it to the actors, so that it becomes a living artifact that others can see, understand, remember, be changed by.

The conductor's questions structure the telling of the story so that essential information is revealed as economically as possible. We need to know the very basic things—where the event took place, when, who was there, what happened. For some tellers, this is obvious enough; for others, it's part of a process of bringing what may be a rather diffuse experience into focus.

"I always feel like I'm a bit outside the action, kind of an onlooker. I think I've felt like this since I was a little kid."

"Tell us about one time when you felt like this. Where were you?"

"Um, let's see. I guess last week, at my uncle's retirement party."

Now we have the germ of a story. The conductor can find out what happened at Uncle Neil's party, and the enactment of this moment will have echoes of all the other times the teller has felt this way.

The actors need to hear the specifics so that they will know what to do when the scene starts. And the story itself needs these concrete features in order to embody its meaning in a coherent shape. Without basic information about what happened, when and where and with whom, the story loses its way in confusion and abstraction.

So one of the conductor's first questions is likely to be "Where does this story take place?" soon followed by a "when" question, like "How old were you?" At the same time, the conductor expands the interview outward by asking the teller to pick actors for the emerging key roles. Sometimes the teller looks up surprised at this point. He's forgotten about the actors. But from this moment on, he and the audience will be anticipating the action that will soon take place in front of them.

As the conductor's questions help ground the story in time and place, they also are calling forth the teller's own sense of story. The conductor might ask "What's a title for your story?" or "Where does this story end?" The teller might not have thought of his experience in these terms until now. But when he's invited to, suddenly he sees how this piece of his life does indeed have a shape to it, a beginning and an end and a meaning. His creativity may be further awoken by a question addressed to his imagination: "We know you weren't actually there at the time, but what do you imagine Dr. Fusco did when he read your letter?"

When the teller has chosen an actor for a role in the story, the conductor usually asks the teller for a word to describe this person—not appearance, but inner quality. It's especially important for characters other than the teller, because the story won't necessarily reveal a lot of information about these supporting roles. The teller's "one word"—often two or three—helps the actor get a handle on the role and adds greatly to the authenticity of the scene. Sometimes the teller's word is surprising, giving an unexpected slant to the story. A woman picked someone to play her mother who had come to be with her after a family tragedy. Her words for her mother were "cool, distant." Without this information, the actor would probably have played the mother with conventional motherly warmth and concern. Knowing what the mother was like helped us all understand more about the teller and the poignancy of her experience.

Sometimes the teller's word for a character—or herself—provides a perfect segue into the heart of the story.

"A word for *me* in the story? Oh, I was shocked!"

"What were you shocked about?"

As the story emerges, the conductor begins to sense its dimensions of meaning. Sometimes they are quite apparent, sometimes more hidden. The conductor may need to follow her own vein of curiosity, to be the "naive enquirer" as Australian Playback director Mary Good describes this facet of the conductor's role[1]. What we are looking for is some contrast, some tension between the elements that has made this experience stand out for the teller, perhaps one that she has learned from.

A boy told a story about how his father had come to his birthday party. It seemed to be simply a happy moment that he was recalling. I asked him about other birthdays. It turned out that this was the *only* birthday on which he had ever seen his father. That was where the urgency of the story

---

[1] Mary Good, *The Playback Conductor: Or, How Many Arrows Will I Need?* (unpublished thesis, 1986).

lay, why it called to be told.

On the other hand, the conductor should also recognize that a very simple story may well be complete as the teller tells it. You certainly don't always need to search for more intensity, like the misguided conductor who encrusted a small pearl of a story with layer after layer of "psychological" details.

The essence of the story gives us a core around which to build its shape. It serves as an organizing principle that can bring not only coherence but great depth to the scene. The conductor's aesthetic sense of story will be one of the most important factors in the success of the scene—success in terms of both art and human truth, inseparable as they are in this work.

Of course, it is not simply up to the conductor. The actors are also listening intently. You know, especially with a practiced team, that they will enrich the enactment with their empathic and artistic inspiration. Trusting this, you might leave a good deal of space for them to choose who and what to portray. Sometimes conductors leave it entirely up to the actors to decide what roles to take, instead of asking the teller to choose. But while the actors gain artistic freedom, they lose the richness of the teller's intuitive choice process. A creative compromise is to have the teller choose actors for the two or three main roles. Then the other actors can fill out the scene with roles suggested by their own understanding of its meaning.

As theatre artists, the team will look for any elements that may enhance the dramatic impact of the story. Often this will mean providing some kind of preamble or contrast to the main action. In a story about a woman on a business trip talking long-distance to her husband and being distracted by the noisy lovemaking of a couple in the next room, the conductor set up the scene so that three locations were represented simultaneously—the teller's hotel room, the lovers' room next door, and the bedroom back home with her husband cozily surrounded by the household pets. The scene was rich with resonance and contrast between these three places. We saw the sensuality of the lovers, the different sensuality of the husband with his cats and dogs romping around him, the solitariness of the teller and the hint of her own sexual longing.

Awareness both of meaning and theatrical options will determine how to use non-human roles in a scene. An actor might portray any object or animal that is centrally important to the story's essence. The decision to do this may be either the actor's or the conductor's initiative. In a scene about a man who has to abandon an old blue Chevy that he's driven since he was a college student, an actor plays the car, bringing it to life and even using dialogue. If the story was about a journey where the vehicle itself was not a focus of the teller's experience, we would not need an actor in the role.

How much does the conductor direct the actors at the end of the interview? As little as possible—depending on how experienced they are. Handing over the story to the actors is a ritual moment, a dramatic launch into the next stage. At this transition, the conductor may actually recapitulate the key elements of the story—"We'll see Mario deciding to leave his home, then his loneliness as an immigrant, and then the moment in the park when he hears the melody of his childhood again. Let's watch." If the actors were new to Playback or to each other, they'd probably need this much reminding—or more—about the content and sequence of the story, and possible some suggestions for staging. Even with inexperienced actors, though, the conductor needs to be careful not to retell the story so fully that there's nothing for the actors to add. The conductor, actors, and musician are partners in fulfilling the scene. As Playback practitioner and teacher James Lucal says, "everyone is responsible for the whole story."

With a more experienced team, instead of mentioning details you might say something like: "This is the story of a circle between the past and the present. Let's watch." Or even just "This is Mario's story. Let's watch." As the conductor you gauge how much support the actors need from you. Beyond that, the most important thing is to let everyone feel the fullness of the moment through your manner and your language, the simple, evocative, deliberate language of the storyteller.

Putting It All Together

Carolyn starts telling her story even before she sits down in the teller's chair.

"It's about a recurring nightmare that I have. I had it again this morning."

I slow her down a little, asking her to pick the main roles as they emerge, guiding the telling of her story so that the essential details come out in as few words as possible, and we're not deluged with so much information that there's nothing left for the actors to do.

In the dream, Carolyn is in a strange circular tunnel, rather like a subway station. She is expecting to meet her son. He's not there, and no matter where she looks she can't find him.

"What are you most afraid of?"

"That I'll never see him again."

I ask her a question that comes from my own curiosity. "In the dream, what do you imagine Ryan is feeling?" Carolyn looks a little blank until I give her some alternatives.

"I mean, do you think he's just forgetful, or has he run away on purpose, or is he scared too?"

"Oh, he's terrified, like me."

This helps us to get further into the story. It turns out that Carolyn somehow knows that Ryan has been kidnapped. The kidnapper doesn't actually appear in the dream, but I know we need him—or her—onstage.

"Pick someone to be this kidnapper. Is it a man or a woman? What is this person like?"

Carolyn hasn't really thought about this before, but when she's asked to, the character is vivid in her imagination.

"It's a man. He's cruel, just horrible. He doesn't care how frightened Ryan is."

The story is taking shape in my mind. Carolyn has told us enough. I look over at the actors. They're counting on me to sum up the story. But I know I don't need to say much.

"We'll start in Carolyn's room here at the hotel," I say. I know from experience that it will help actors, audience, and teller to be drawn into the dream if we begin in waking reality. And ending the same way will not only provide artistic unity, it will help Carolyn to return to the here-and-now in a comfortable and safe way.

I recapitulate the elements of the story, very briefly. Then I turn to Carolyn. "So our job is over for now, Carolyn." I look around at the audience too. "Let's watch!"

This is the moment when the action is handed over to the actors. It's not always easy to do this, relinquishing the position of control until the enactment is over. But now is the conductor's time just to be receptive, and to be present with the teller, whatever her needs and responses might be during the scene. Generally, the conductor does not intervene in an enactment, even if she feels that the actors are getting it all wrong, even if the teller is complaining or adding new information. There will always be a chance to comment or make changes once the scene is over.

This time, though, the actors do a wonderful job. We see

the casual goodnights in the hotel room, the tired but happy reminiscences about the evening's festivities. Then, as a low drum beats softly, the teller's actor rises from her bed. She's in the dream. She calls her son's name. On the other side of the stage, the kidnapper approaches the little boy.

"Come with me, Ryan, come with me." The actor playing Ryan resists. The kidnapper becomes more menacing. "Come with me. Your mother won't care. She doesn't really love you anyway." He grabs Ryan and forces him away. The mother continues to call for him. Her anguish grows as she searches in vain. Her voice rises in a crescendo of panic, until finally she wakes up in her hotel bed. Her roommate tries to comfort her.

"Oh god, what a dream," says the teller's actor. "Why on earth am I dreaming this again?" She leaps out of bed. "Amy, I'll be right back. I've got to call him."

Beside me, the teller reacts in surprise. "That's just what I did," she whispers to me, even though this particular detail hadn't emerged in the interview.

The scene ends. I ask Carolyn if it felt like her story. "It certainly did," she says. She puts her hand over her heart. "Phew!"

It seems to me that this scene may call for a transformation. If we were doing a full-length show, I could let subsequent stories speak to whatever is unresolved in this one. But today there's only time for one.

"In Playback Theatre," I say, "we can change the way things happened. Is there some other way you'd like to see this story end?"

She doesn't hesitate. "Yes! I'd like to find him, safe."

Sometimes tellers don't want to change stories, even apparently traumatic or unfinished experiences. Sometimes they can't think of an alternative scenario. We don't supply a transformation ourselves, or solicit it from the audience.

It must come from the teller's own spontaneity. When it does, it can be a powerfully redemptive experience, not only for the teller but for everyone present. It is not simply a "happy ending" that we are invoking: it is the primary creative power of the individual to be the author of his or her own experience.

Carolyn tells us how she wants to change the dream. There won't be any kidnapper. Ryan has simply lost track of time because he's having so much fun with his friend.

We re-do the scene, this time with the audience playing the role of neighbors who help Carolyn in her search. Finally she's reunited with her son. She's overcome with relief, and the awareness of how precious he is to her—and she's annoyed, too. But they hug, and once again the scene comes to a close.

Carolyn is pleased with this new version of her experience. Again she's surprised by one of the details—"How did they know that Ryan builds forts all the time?" It's one of the benefits of having ordinary people as actors, people who might be parents themselves, who share in many of the personal dramas that tellers tell.

It takes time and practice to be able to fulfill all the facets of the conductor's role and to flow smoothly between them in performance. When we teach conducting we encourage people to focus on the aspects that come most easily to them—usually the relationships with the teller and the story—before trying to master it all. Whatever your particular strengths or challenges as a conductor, you will eventually be rewarded with the awareness that your well-rounded skill has helped audience, tellers and fellow performers find the satisfying experience they seek in Playback.

6

Music for Playback

Let's look at another scene, this time paying special attention to the music.

"This is kind of a travelling story. I really love to travel, and my husband and I used to travel a lot before our daughter was born. And everywhere we would go, I would want to stay there. Ireland, New Mexico, London—they all seemed like the most wonderful places to live, while I was there. Now we're about to go on a trip to Vancouver, and Avery is nervous that it'll happen again—I'll want to move there permanently. But I recently realized that I feel different now. I'm really happy where I am. I love my house and my family and my work. I think I can finally enjoy other places without being tempted to uproot myself."

As the actors slowly prepare themselves and the stage, the musician plays short phrases on the recorder. The melody built around minor thirds suggests a feeling of longing.

The actors are in position. The music stops. Helen and Avery begin a whirlwind tour around the stage, stopping to dance with the actor who is playing Ireland, then someone else vividly costumed as the American Southwest. Now the musician is at the keyboard, playing a merry waltz reminiscent of the recorder melody, but in a major key. At each point, when it's time to leave, Helen resists.

"Let's move to Dublin, Avery!" she says. "We could live

This chapter is based on my article, "Music in Playback Theatre," which appeared in *The Arts in Psychotherapy*, 19, (1992). The musical terminology used here will add meaning for some readers but is not essential for understanding what I am saying about the use of music.

in one of these quaint little houses and go to the pub every evening." Avery drags her away. As they continue their journey, the keyboard music slows down, changing back into the minor. Helen looks longingly over her shoulder at each place they leave.

The first part of the scene comes to an end. Marking the transition to the second part, the musician plays a variation of the first theme, again on the recorder. Now Helen is in her house, getting ready to leave for Vancouver. She looks around her. The musician is playing soft, sustained chords on the keyboard. The open harmonies rest on a deep bass note.

"Goodbye, house," says Helen. "I'll be back. I'll miss you." She joins Avery, and they dance away, joyfully, free of struggle this time. Staying with the same chords, the musician introduces a gentle rhythm. Over it, he sings "I will come home...."

Music in Theatre

Music has a unique power to express our emotional experience. A few notes of music can sometimes touch our hearts more deeply and more quickly than any words could. Like our own inner worlds, music is composed of shifting, kaleidoscopic patterns and transformations that have a direction and logic that we recognize even if we cannot articulate it.

It is this fundamental connection between music and emotion that invites the use of music in theatre. As every film and theater director knows, music can evoke a mood or heighten dramatic action with great effectiveness. Unless it is used in a way that's too predictable or in some way distasteful, we're likely to find ourselves caught by the music and drawn into the action.

In Playback Theatre, where subjective emotional realities hold center stage, the music has a particularly important role to play.[2] It has the capacity to create an atmosphere, shape the scene, and, above all, convey the emotional development of the story. The musician is an essential participant in the Playback team's basic task of building a fragment of theatre that honors someone's real-life experience.

Music for Playback Theatre has its own challenges, its own precepts and techniques, distinct from the use of music in scripted theatre, and from other musical performance modes. Like the acting, the music is a gift to the teller and the audience, not a vehicle for virtuosity. At the end of a performance, you might wistfully feel, if you're the musician, that few audience members actually paid attention to your creative and sensitive playing. Your satisfaction must come from the knowledge that music's power is all the more because it works whether or not it is noticed. Your music is a constant element throughout the show, supporting, shaping, enriching everything that happens.

Music at the Beginning of a Performance

Music has a special role to play in the ritual and ceremonial aspects of a Playback performance, in addition to its expressive function during the scenes themselves. So music is likely to be part of the show's opening, focusing the audience's attention and announcing that we are entering a realm that is distinct from everyday life. The musician might play a short instrumental solo, or perhaps lead a musical improvisation with the actors singing or playing percussion instruments. The conductor and musician may alternate words and music in an opening invocation to the audience.

When it's time to move into action, beginning with some

---

[2] In spite of the value of music in Playback, it is certainly possible to work effectively without music if necessary, especially in non-performance contexts.

fluid sculptures, the purpose of the music shifts slightly, moving from the ceremonial to the expressive mode. Now the music is there to enhance the dramatic impact of the fluid sculptures. Like the incremental action of each actor, the music you play will influence the growing shape of the sculpture. You are responding to what you see, the actors respond to what they are hearing from you. When it's time to end, the music can help them round off the action in a dramatically coordinated way, with perhaps a sustained chord, or the quiet "ting" of a Tibetan bell.

Music in the Scenes: The Setting-Up

As soon as the interview between the conductor and teller is over, signalled by the conductor's "Watch!", the musician begins to play music as the actors silently prepare the stage. This setting-up music may be neutral in tone, or it may hint at what is to come by setting a specific mood—ominous, lyrical, comical, etc. In a scene in which the teller as a child was shocked to witness her sister having a seizure, the setting-up music began with a long, high note on the violin. This note finally slid downwards in pitch, leading into a tuneless little tune played without the warmth of vibrato. The alarming, rather nightmare-like effect of this music came back at the climax of the scene, as we watched the teller's actor react in horror to her sister's seizure.

One of the most important things going on during the setting-up is the transition into theatre from the here-and-now dialogue between teller and conductor. The music is helping to create a kind of trance in the audience. They are led into a space where they can fully enter the world that the actors are about to conjure onstage.

"We'll do one more story." A man comes to the stage. He

86

tells us that he was diagnosed with AIDS two years ago. Then, a year later, his lover became ill. The teller lives through his lover's illness and death. The audience is hushed, deeply moved by this man's story and his courage to tell it publicly. "Watch!" says the conductor. As the actors begin to move into position, the musician strikes a large gong. The sound is loud, reverberant, shocking, uncompromising.

For the actors, the setting-up music has a pragmatic role: it ends when you as the musician see that everyone is positioned and ready to begin. It's a useful cue to any actors who may not be able to see the whole stage. And it allows the enactment to begin crisply. One moment everyone is quiet and still: the next moment the action has begun.

In performances where the actors confer together before beginning a scene, the music during the setting-up may be heard in a different way. I was puzzled to hear some Playback musicians in Australia talking about their frustration at not being listened to by the audience. As they talked, I realized that they were referring to a situation which I'd never experienced, even though I had been playing music for Playback for many years. In their companies' performances, the interview was followed by an actors' huddle. For the musicians, this was a time when they could play without having to trim their music to the action on stage—a moment when they could spread their musical wings. But what tended to happen was that the audience, taking their cue from the actors whispering together at the back of the stage, would chat to each other, not only ignoring but almost drowning out the poor musician. Then, when the actors were ready to begin, the audience would again become quiet and attentive.

In contrast, when the actors set up silently, without discussion, the audience is caught up in the taut mystery of that moment. They're already entranced. It is a time when, because of the audience's focussed attention, the music can in fact be very subtle and understated rather than a full-fledged improvisational overture.

During the Enactment

Once the scene is underway, you make choices about which elements to focus on, when to play, what instruments to use, etc. You may decide to play music to heighten the experience of the teller; for example, playing fast, chaotic phrases as the teller's actor runs frantically from one obligation to another. On the other hand, sometimes you might play music that expresses a dimension not represented by one of the actors. Perhaps the teller hinted at an underlying feeling, and the teller's actor is playing the way he behaved rather than how he felt. At the conclusion of a scene about being harshly punished at a Boy Scout camp, the music expressed Charlie's feelings of pain and humiliation, in contrast to the face-saving bravado portrayed by the teller's actor.

In this case, the music also reminded us of an emotional reality which the actor had expressed at an earlier moment in the scene. The musical theme was a tag signifying an element that we had already seen. As well as intensifying the mood, this kind of repetition also strengthens the aesthetic unity of the scene.

With a change or intensification in what you are playing, the music can be used to help move the scene into its climax. It can be surprisingly powerful to simply stop. Actors will almost invariably respond to a sudden silence by moving the scene toward whatever needs to happen next. Slowing the music, playing final-sounding cadences, or recapitulating a theme can help to coordinate an ending.

Scott told a story about his life-long relationship with

his alcoholic father. The conductor decided to stage this scene in three chronological parts. Without the benefit of a script or a curtain to retire behind, the actors were able to begin and end these mini-scenes effectively with the help of the music. Between each scene, the musician played major VII chords on the guitar, articulating them differently each time, but returning always to the same instrument and chord progression. The music framed and linked these short scenes, giving continuity and structure to the whole enactment.

It's often appropriate to stage scenes in parts, as this one was. Helen's story, at the beginning of this chapter, was another. Music can be an economical and aesthetic way of managing the staging gracefully. As well as assisting the actors, this transitional music tells the audience that one part has ended, the next is about to begin.

In transformation scenes, the challenge for the musician as well as the actors is to make the redemptive re-enactment as powerful as the original scene. For both actors and musician, it's usually easier to play an unhappy scene with great impact than it is to be fully dramatic in a "happy ending." Changing instruments at this point is one way to add freshness and effect.

Sometimes the musician's most effective instrument is the voice. Even if you're not a polished singer, the voice has a unique immediacy and pathos for the hearer. When words are added, the impact can be still stronger—if the words are well-chosen. It is a delicate, complex task. You're composing a song on the spot, keeping in mind the needs of the teller, the actors, and the theatrical aspects of the scene. You need to distill language like a poet, so as not to be trite or obvious. These phrases will usually work best if they are extremely simple, perhaps just a repeated key phrase, or name.

How much music does there need to be? It can vary a great deal. It certainly doesn't need to be constant, and will have more effect if it is heard at judiciously selected moments. Like the actors, you use your artistic sense of timing, pacing, silence.

In a scene about an almost-accident on the road, the enactment begins without music. Then, as the teller swerves to miss by inches a car speeding straight toward her, there is a volley of drumbeats, followed by a rhythm like the wild beating of the teller's heart as she realizes how close she has come to death.

The Playback musician is not in the business of sound-effects. Most of the time, it is the emotional dimension that the music is expressing, one way or another. In scenes which seem superficial and anecdotal, it might be hard to get ideas about what you could play, and you might decide to contribute sound effects rather than play nothing. However, if you open yourself to inspiration, even in such an apparently barren situation, you may find yourself playing something that influences the dynamic of the whole show and invites a deeper level of storytelling.

Working With the Actors

As the musician, you are very much part of the Playback team, and as we saw earlier, you need to be a storyteller like everyone else. All the musical possibilities I've mentioned so far depend on your sense of story, and your mutual relationship with the actors. The music is far more than an accompaniment. When the collaboration is functioning well, the music becomes like another actor on stage, involved in an exchange of cues with everyone else, each enhancing the others' ability to render the story as vividly, truthfully, and artistically as they can.

You must be sensitive to the need for dialogue to be clearly heard, playing softly or in counterpoint with spoken lines so as not to obscure the actors' words—except for those times when drowning out the dialogue may actually intensify the drama. At the right moments, an escalation of volume in the music can prompt the actors' voices to rise also, conveying conflict or excitement even as the words themselves become indistinguishable. In one unforgettable story about a failed attempt to escape from Communist Romania, the climax comes when the teller and his two friends are caught by armed police. Over the shouts of rage, terror, and despair, the musician plays a frantic, abrasive crescendo on the tambourine. The music, smothering the actors' cries, provides an analogue to the theme of suppression and desperation.

This kind of co-creativity depends on a healthy mutual trust and respect, without which the actors and musician may find themselves feeling competitive rather than cooperative. The musicians I mentioned earlier who were frustrated during the setting-up also spoke of feeling that at times they had to struggle to find a place for their music during the enactments. I've sometimes experienced this absence of shared vision when playing music with a newly-formed group, or with people who have just come together at a workshop. It's a matter of knowing what the synergy between you can be like, and having the time and commitment to achieve it.

Teamwork is especially important in those moments when music by itself can best carry the meaning. At such times, the actors can pause and let the music take center stage. Spoken language and movement may seem too finite: strong feeling can sometimes be more effectively expressed in music's direct call to the emotional imagination.

In a performance that happens to take place on Mother's Day, a woman tells the story of her daughter's first childbirth.

She's an amusing raconteur.

"And who else was present at the birth, Shelly?"

"The sperm donor," she says, letting us know her opinion of her daughter's partner. The audience chuckles as the "baby" is born. The actors, well aware of the profound meaning of the story, wait for the laughter to subside as the scene draws to a close. They hold their positions, indicating that it's not over yet. In this space, the musician plays soft arpeggiated guitar chords, singing a lyrical melody with the words "My baby...my baby." Shelly's amused distance from the scene vanishes. She leans against the conductor's shoulder, her mouth trembling, tears in her eyes.

Working With the Conductor

Close cooperation between musician and conductor will strengthen the performance. Sitting there on either side of the stage, your roles are in some ways parallel. You share a special responsibility to support the actors and shape the story. When your partnership is strong and mutually trusting, it can be like an axis for the whole ensemble, creating the optimal conditions for the story to be realized. Your tasks in the process are sequential. The conductor's directorial role is suspended once the enactment has begun; and it is the musician who, to some degree, assumes this function through the shaping influence of the music. Some of your artistic decisions may follow on from the conductor's suggestions for staging--for example, to do a scene in three parts, or to let a certain element be represented by the music.

This conductor-musician partnership can also create an aesthetic framework for the whole show. You might weave music through the conductor's beginning invocation to the audience, play again in a musical interlude that helps people breathe again after a particularly intense scene, and then end the evening with a closure that's both musical and verbal.

Music and Lighting

If your company uses lights, the musician and the lighting person work together to maximize the effect of these two elements. Lighting for Playback Theatre is another non-cognitive way of telling the story. The audience's responses will be strongly affected by changes in the amount and coloration of the light, though they may be hardly aware of it. Like the musician, the lighting person is tracking the emotional development of the story. The effectiveness of both is enhanced when you work together to underscore a crucial element or shape the progress of a scene. (See next chapter.)

The Musician's Skills

A number of Playback musicians that I know about—including myself—are also practicing music therapists. It's not a coincidence. The skills you draw on for this kind of playing are similar to those required for music therapy. Playback musicians need to be able to play fluently and creatively, preferably on more than one instrument; they need to be very comfortable with improvisation; they need to be confident enough of their musicianship to have no hesitation in translating their perceptions and impulses into music. It's helpful if you're versatile enough to be able to suggest a variety of musical styles, both instrumentally and vocally, if required by the story—classical, blues, rap, ethnic, children's, etc. Although Playback music most often relates to mood in a way that bypasses specific cultural association, there are times when the suggestion of a recognizable musical style can be very effective. For instance, we once did a scene about a personal breakthrough that happened at a camp for traditional fiddle and dance. Playing my violin fiddle-style helped with the authenticity and emotional impact of that enactment.

But music skills are not the only important thing. The musician also needs the capacity to attune to the teller and to fellow company members, the ability to respond flexibly to the needs of the scene—and an acceptance of the essentially humble nature of this work. Just as the actors must be prepared to be picked for a difficult or limited role, or not picked at all, a Playback musician must be equally ready to play expansively and boldly, or to play hardly at all in a scene which may offer little scope for music.

Both musician and actor in Playback Theatre are called upon to combine a therapist's empathy and non-judgmental openness with a readiness for expressiveness. Not every technically-skilled performer, by any means, is mature and centered enough for this work.

On the other hand, since these qualities of openness, empathy, generosity, and spontaneity are at least as important as actual music skills, someone who is untrained can be unexpectedly successful playing music for a scene. It's a question of spontaneity and courage. Everyone has a voice; anyone can use simple percussion instruments. And these tools can be enough to create truly moving and dramatic music for a Playback scene. Obviously, the more music skills you have, the more choices you have in Playback music. But it's very valuable for everyone, musician or not, to experience the musician's role—in rehearsals or workshops, if not in actual performance. You may be surprised at the effect your music can have. And trying out the musician's role will certainly raise your awareness of the music when you're back in your customary role of actor or conductor.

Instruments

If you're a trained musician, your main instrument is the
one on which you'll have the most expressive power, whether
it's a keyboard, a stringed or wind instrument, or percussion.
You can complement it with an array of other instruments
to provide a variety of timbre, pitch range, volume, melodic
and rhythmic capacity, and cultural or emotional connota-
tion. These instruments can include almost anything, from
familiar rhythm band-type instruments to exotic instruments
to homemade or found objects. In an impromptu situation,
or where there's no budget for "real" instruments, pots, pans,
wooden spoons, and kazoos could supply a variety of sounds
and effects. If you're buying instruments, a serviceable collection might include a low-pitched, resonant drum, cabasa,
slide-whistle or kazoo, bamboo flute or recorder, woodblock,
xylophone, and various bells, in addition to a more complex
main instrument. The voice is an always-available instrument
that can be extremely powerful in Playback music, with or
without accompaniment.

The Cabasa and the Sea

*A man tells a childhood story about building a sand castle
by the sea with another little boy. They got into a fight, and
while they struggled together, the unnoticed tide washed away
the sand castle.*

*One actor is chosen to portray the sea. Kneeling at the
edge of the stage, draped in a gauzy blue cloth, she moves in a
gentle, regular motion, never drawing the focus away from the
actors playing the two little boys. The musician accompanies
her movement with a quiet, sibilant rhythm on the cabasa. The
waves gradually engulf the sand castle. The boys stop fighting,
their conflict forgotten in their loss. In the silence, the cabasa*

music continues, indifferent and constant as the waves them-selves.

7

Presence, Presentation, and Ritual

Playback Theatre is intimate, informal, unpretentious, and accessible. But it *is* theatre: we are consciously entering an arena that is different from day-to-day reality. To create the heightened atmosphere necessary to any theatrical event, we draw on *presence*, the performers' carefully focused demeanor and attention; *presentation*, the care taken with the physical, structural, and visual aspects of the performance; and *ritual*, the patterns that provide a consistent framework throughout the performance and from one show to another. Through presence, presentation, and ritual, the message is conveyed that these personal stories, these lives, are worthy of our attention and respect.

The Playback paradox of formality and intimacy is encapsulated in a moment at the beginning of one show. The actors enter the stage one at a time. They say their names and tell the audience something about themselves, whatever comes to them in the moment.

"I'm Eve, and today I wrote to a friend who's been on my mind for quite a while."

Eve is speaking simply as herself, as one person to another; she hasn't rehearsed or even planned this statement; and the audience hears it as the unmediated communication that it is. But at the same time, they are receiving her words in the context of the ritual pattern and presence of the actors' entrance. This different message tells them that this is not just Eve chatting to them; this is a performance, with forms, structures, and intentions. Most of all, it says that Eve's private experience merits communication in this public context, and that you, the audience, are invited to offer your stories in the same way.

When you watch a Playback Theatre performance, you respond to its heightened, ritualized quality. If it were not there, you would feel its absence. And yet it is one of the hardest things to talk about and teach. We are unused to paying attention to such things in our Western industrial culture. Generally, the elements of ritual and presentation are managed poorly in community events that call for them, moments of transition or celebration like a funeral, a graduation, a piano recital. (An exception that I am aware of is in New Zealand, where the Maori, masters of graceful and functional ceremony, have had a significant influence in this respect on the culture at large. Public occasions, from PTA meetings to official ceremonies, are now likely to be built around ritual structures based in traditional Maori custom. New Zealanders have found that these forms support the purposes for which they have come together—to hear and understand each other, to honor the past and celebrate new beginnings.) In Playback, new practitioners are often perplexed by the challenge of learning how to use ritual, how to perform with presence and conscious presentation.

Presence

Simply by the way they stand, move, listen, relate to one another, the actors can communicate either that they fully understand the depth and power of what they are doing—or the opposite. I've often seen actors, usually but not always new to Playback, whose casualness onstage undercuts the work they are there to do. They certainly don't realize the effect they are creating. I think that their lack of presence most likely comes from not understanding the impact of their demeanor, and also, perhaps, a shyness about presenting themselves onstage in full command of their presence.

On the other hand, actors who have mastered this aspect of performance can greatly deepen Playback's effect. It's both simple and subtle—the difference between sitting straight or slumped on the boxes, between standing alert and poised or fidgeting as you wait for the interview to be finished. It's keeping your communications with each other, for example before pairs, to a sparse minimum and avoiding the temptation to interact unnecessarily with each other, physically or verbally. The most effective Playback actors have a Zen-like attention and self-discipline.

The setting-up is a moment where the actors' presence plays an especially important part. As we've seen, this is a time when the audience can be led into a trance, into a place of utmost receptiveness to our creativity. The more disciplined the actors are in this moment, the more the audience will be drawn into this magical meeting place. Even if the actors huddle, either to plan the enactment or just to attune before launching into action, they can do so with concentration and control, not losing the flow of the ritual.

At the close of the scene, there is again scope for the actors to maintain their focused presence. In the challenging moment of the acknowledgment, it takes courage to look at the teller with all of yourself, with your actor's dignity. If you can do it, you have enriched the gift that you are now offering to the teller. Then, returning to the boxes, you keep that focus, you show with your body and your face that you are ready to give yourself fully to the next story.

The conductor, more than anyone else, sets the tone for the kind of presence that will distinguish this performance from a completely informal gathering. Standing on the stage at the beginning of a show, all eyes on him, the responsibility of the evening on his shoulders, the conductor can either meet this moment or shrink from it. If he can fulfill his role with presence, from beginning to end, the audience and the actors will join him in the co-creation of a genuinely theatrical event.

Presentation—The Stage

The ideal space for a Playback Theatre performance is a small (100 seats or fewer), intimate theatre with a stage that is raised just enough to allow clear sight lines, perhaps one or two feet higher than the floor, with steps to provide easy access. Or it could be an arena theatre where the audience's seats descend level by level to the stage area. Playback does not work well on a proscenium stage and has no need of a curtain. The important qualities are intimacy and accessibility to the stage. The acoustics should be bright enough so that speech, even a teller's quiet voice, can easily be heard, but not so bright that clarity is lost in reverberation.

However, as we've seen, the "stage" in a Playback performance is very often not a stage at all, but part of a room where the furniture has been cleared away. All the more reason to take care with how it is set up. With or without an actual stage, we need to create a physical space in which the stories can come to life.

The basic set-up of the stage area is very simple. On the audience's left—stage right—two chairs are placed side by side, angled in toward the center, for the conductor and the teller. For the first part of the show, the teller's chair is empty. The audience's attention may not be directly drawn to it. But on some level they notice, and wonder: "Who sits in that other chair?" On the other side of the stage is the musician's seat and a collection of instruments spread out on a low table or a cloth on the floor. Across the back is a row of crates or wooden boxes for the actors to sit on and later use as props during the scene. (It's traditional in Playback Theatre to use plastic milk crates for this purpose—amazingly similar and available all around the world. They're cheap, or free, lightweight and stackable, although not exactly comfortable to sit on. There's a Playback joke that you can always tell Playback actors by their corrugated rear ends.)

On one side, usually stage right, set back a little, there is the prop tree, a wooden structure hung with pieces of cloth of many colors and textures. This is the most colorful thing on the stage, evocative and aesthetic in itself. Although your actual use of the props is likely to be minimal, the prop tree contributes a festive, theatrical presence. The props can be chosen and arranged with this in mind. You can search for fabric that is striking and appealing and varied. You can hang the pieces with artistic awareness—the long black one next to the lacy red, the fish net against the bold metallic, and so on.

These simple objects define the empty space within, the space which will be filled with stories as yet unknown.

The Room

When the Playback Theatre event is taking place in a room that is not usually used for performance, there are steps we can take to make the most out of whatever space we find ourselves in.

One of the first things we can do is to arrange the chairs in accordance with Playback's purposes of connection and communication. In the traditional theatre, the audience usually sits in straight lines. Awareness of each other is kept to a minimum, so that they can more fully enter into of the imagined reality of the actors, undistracted by the real people beside them. In Playback Theatre, we want people to be as aware of each other as they are of the created world onstage. We want them to feel the phenomenon of their sharing in this event, of which the enacted story is one part. We place the chairs in curving rows so that audience members can see each other, and so our presence in the stage area completes a kind of circle.[1] We make sure there is an aisle down the middle so that anyone can easily walk to the stage area. We may place cushions in front of the front row for children or others who want to be sure of a good view. We try to make everything as comfortable and attractive as possible. We want people, walking in, to feel welcome and pleased to be there.

It is amazing how quickly and easily you can transform a space along these lines. In just a few minutes, with some of you setting up the stage and others arranging chairs and cushions, an ordinary, even unwelcoming room can become inviting and theatrical.

Lights

Whether in a theatre or an informal room, stage lights will make a huge difference, further defining the space and bathing everything in colors far from the prosaic fluorescent or white lighting that people are used to. Playback lighting is different from traditional stage lighting, usually characterized by brilliant points of focus and the attempt to simulate specific environments. Instead, lighting for a Playback show will mostly be a matter of moody, impressionistic washes of color that change with the fluidity of emotion.

A basic set of lights for Playback might include two large scoop lights for overall color, together with perhaps four spots or fresnels for more focused effects. Each light is filtered through a gel so there is a repertoire of colors to

---

[1]For related reasons, the conductor often invites audience members to introduce themselves to someone sitting near them, so that they are from then on aware of sitting with people whose faces they have looked into and whose voices they have heard. In a room where the seating is fixed, and so cannot be rearranged in curving rows, these audience introductions are especially important.

be used according to the needs of the scene. The lights are mounted on poles and controlled by rheostat plugs set into a light box at the back of the room. The lighting person—another storytelling member of the team—helps to frame the story by lowering the lights after the interview and again at the end of the story. Throughout the enactment, he or she provides subtle alterations in lighting as the drama develops. Before the show, the lights can be carefully positioned so that the teller and the conductor will be well-lit during both the interview and the scene. It is here, especially in the teller's face, that some of the most riveting drama takes place.

Not all groups or all performances use lights; they're more bulky and expensive than any of the other equipment. Even without stagelights, though, there is often some way that you can improve on the lighting that's there. Some overhead lights can be turned off; perhaps there are lamps that can be brought in to provide color and focus.

What to Wear

Part of the performers' presentation is their clothing. Every company's solution to this question is different, depending on their own sense of style and appropriateness. What they all have in common is the need to wear clothes that allow the actors to move easily and are as neutral as possible, so you can more readily be seen as a grandmother, a frog, a policeman, or the moon. Whether you decide to wear nothing but black, or coordinated solid colors, or just street clothes, you will need to choose garments that give you maximum flexibility to move and express.

Beginnings and Endings

The importance of presentation extends to the manner

of the performance itself. For instance, there's room for a great deal of care and creativity in the way you begin and end the show. Everything you do, from the moment you first appear, will either enhance or undercut the theatrical impact. Whether you dance into the room playing percussion instruments, or open with a meditative vocal improvisation, or make statements like Eve's, following them with momentary one-person sculptures, or any other of the infinite possibilities, the show will move smoothly into the Playback process from an opening that is both theatrical and authentically human. (Once, in our boldest early days, we began a show by changing into our performing clothes on stage, behind a screen, two at a time. The audience had no idea what to make of this outrageousness. It certainly was dramatic, but on reflection we felt that it hadn't really achieved anything useful.)

When it's all over, your ending will also help to affirm the meaning and dignity of what everyone has just shared. It's another moment that's easy to duck. But it is important, nevertheless, to stand together, to receive the audience's applause with a bow, perhaps applauding them back, and to leave the stage with presence—even if you return a minute later to meet the audience informally.

Ritual

In Playback Theatre, ritual means the repeated structures in space and time that provide stability and familiarity, within which can be contained the unpredictable. Ritual also helps to summon the heightened perception of experience that can transform life into theatre.

The presence of ritual is often established even before the show begins. As we've seen, Playback performances very often take place in spaces that are not usually used for theatre. The pragmatic task of setting up the room and the stage, with the boxes and instruments and prop tree, and the two chairs for teller and conductor, is also a ritual. It is a symbolic process of temporarily taking over this lunchroom or whatever it is and making it into something different—a place where stories can be told and heard and seen, where people are invited to be with each other in a new way. If we do not find ourselves in a world that is amenable to the Playback process, we must create it.

Once the show begins, it is the conductor, primarily, who establishes and regulates the rituals of performance. He needs to be fully aware of this shamanistic aspect of his role and to use it responsibly and artistically.

One of the conductor's tools of ritual is his choice of language—throughout the performance, but especially during the interviews. On one level, this language is informal and conversational—"Hi, welcome to the teller's chair. Is this your first time as a teller?" and so on. On another level, the language is formulaic, repetitive, and chosen with a high degree of care and consciousness. Although every interview is different, many of the conductor's questions will recur from one interview to the next. He is likely to guide the interview in certain directions—towards specificity; towards the meanings, sometimes hidden, of the story; towards the teller's own creativity. When the interview is going well, there will be a palpable rhythm of question and response as the teller joins in the ritual.

The conductor is likely to repeat some of the teller's responses, turning to the actors and the audience as he does so. "This is about a dream, although I'm not sure it really was a dream," the teller says. The conductor turns to the audience. "A dream that perhaps wasn't a dream," he says, bringing a slight emphasis to the words. He is making sure that everyone is hearing the story—it's not the teller's job to speak loudly—and he is also immediately heightening the storytelling process through the ritual element of repetition.

When the interview is finished, the conductor's final injunction to the teller and the audience is almost always "Watch!" or, if this seems too abrupt and bossy, "Let's watch!" Making this injunction at the end of every interview is part of the ritual. It serves to set up the scene that is to follow, for the teller, the actors, and the audience. For the teller, it is also a strong suggestion that her active participation is over for the time being.

The actual sequence of the enactment is another place where ritual plays an important part. The enactment follows a pattern of five stages, as we saw in chapter 3. After the interview, there is the highly ritualistic setting-up, then the scene itself, followed by the acknowledgment and the teller's last word. The consistency of this sequence creates a structure within which the scene can take flight. Without the ritual of the five stages, actors, teller, and audience would all be susceptible to feeling confused and insecure.

Music is an essential element in the establishment of ritual. As we discussed in the last chapter, music's ritual effect in Playback Theatre is related to but distinct from its aesthetic, expressive function. I'm not sure if the stabilizing, dignifying effect of the music comes from our cultural familiarity with the use of music in religious and civil ceremonies, or whether there's something inherently ennobling about music that leads to its use at such events. In any case, music, especially at moments of beginning, ending, and transition, will strongly enhance the ritual dimension. At such times, the musician, like the conductor, is consciously fulfilling a shaman-like role.

Stage lights are another adjunct to ritual. The lights go down; people become quiet, receptive, eager. During the scene, the changes in the lighting will continue to place the frame of art around the action. Along with the music, it says "Witness this! This is important!"

I've mentioned earlier the emotionally disturbed children who come regularly to Playback shows, who can never get enough of this opportunity to tell their stories. To help the children deal with their disappointment when they are not chosen as tellers, one of the company members makes use of her ongoing presence as the school psychologist to provide some extra chances for storytelling. Going into the classrooms, she gathers the children in a circle. Those who want to may tell their stories, one at time. After each one, Diana retells the story, adding a touch of ceremony to her telling. The children are satisfied by this. Although it's not the same as seeing their stories acted out, it's different from simply telling something in a private or conversational mode. It is the inclusion of ritual, slight as it is, that raises the telling of personal stories into something satisfying and memorable.

Ritual and Meaning

When we were first exploring the significance of ritual, especially the ritual sequence of enacting a scene, we were invited to take part in a Japanese tea ceremony, to experience what this ancient tradition might have in common with the new tradition we were creating. Although the grace of the tea ceremony did indeed make a lasting impression on us, the truth is our response was lacking in appropriate dignity. We found ourselves hard put to keep our composure in the face of the rather overwrought solemnity of the officiants, amateurs like ourselves. Equally challenging was the presence of the new husband of one of our members, who, we were beginning to learn, had a particular fondness for costume. Eager and dead serious, he showed up at this tea ceremony on a barn floor wearing full Samurai gear, complete with sword.

Although we felt a little ashamed of our struggle with mirth, I think that what we were responding to was a disjuncture between the fact of our neophyte experimentation, on the one hand, and the pretense of connection to a venerable tradition, on the other. There is nothing inherently foolish in participating in the established rituals of another culture. The absurdity was in the failure to acknowledge how new and foreign this was to all of us. None of us, including our hosts, had more than an inkling of the meaning this ceremony carried in its original context.

Rituals exist to embody meaning, even to construct it out of the disparate elements of our experience. They are "frameworks of expectancy."[2] If a ritual is cut adrift from the context in which it was created, if it fails to justify itself in the present moment, it becomes hollow and even ludicrous. The rituals established in Playback have grown out of the needs and meanings of the events in a performance. If they should ever seem meaningless or arbitrary, their reason for existence is over.

The theatre director Peter Brook speaks of theatre's ancient function of providing a temporary reintegration for a community that, like all communities, lives its day-to-day life in fragmentation. But this function of theatre can no longer be fulfilled, he says, because the process of fragmentation has gone so far that we no longer share common touchstones on which rituals can be built. Instead, he says, modern-day actors must find a new "matrix of unity," which is the moment of performance, the *now* shared by actors and audience.[3]

---

[2]M. Douglas, quoted in *Rituals in Families and Family Therapy*, Imber-Black, Roberts, and Whiting, (New York: Norton, 1988), 11.

[3]Peter Brook, "Leaning on the Moment," *Parabola*, 4 (2), (1979): 46-59.

Playback may be a theatre in which this essential "matrix of unity" is created both in the old way and the new way. Although we are often dealing with audiences no less diverse than any other modern audience, and so our shared cultural frame of reference may be no less impoverished, the difference is that our "play" comes from the people's lives. The need for traditional cultural touchstones is less pressing, because we—audience and company together—will find our own within the microcosm of a performance, and they are likely to include the personal triumphs and losses and rueful realizations that transcend specific culture. We perform rituals that are based in the immediate needs of the event itself, neither arbitrary nor ancient nor obscure, but with a readily apparent role to play in the purpose for which we are gathered. At the same time, we are indeed "leaning on the moment"—we are above all sharing in this birth of the scene, this revelation of a life.

8

Playback and Healing

Theatre, says Peter Brook in another article, was created to "reflect the sacred universal mysteries, and also to comfort the drunkard and the lonely man.[1]" (I think he also means the lonely woman and the lonely child.)

Playback Theatre has always been a theatre of comfort, in this sense. A commitment to the flowering of the human spirit was part of Jonathan's original vision, and as we told our own stories in those first years, we learned for ourselves how this could be fulfilled. When we moved our work out into the community, we saw how telling stories and watching them enacted often seemed, at least in the moment, a redemptive experience, no matter what kind of story was told. For some, telling a story in Playback brought catharsis, or simply affirmation; for others, telling a story publicly was an important step toward connection. For groups, it was a way to build bridges, and a way to strengthen or celebrate bonds that may have already been there.

Playback's healing efficacy comes from a number of elements. First of all, as we've seen in earlier chapters, people *need* to tell their stories. It's a basic human imperative. From the telling of our stories comes our sense of identity, and our place in the world, and our compass of the world itself. In the fragmented existence that many of us experience, where there may be little continuity of people and place, where life moves too fast for us to listen carefully to one another, where many people are searching for meaning that seems more than ever elusive, Playback Theatre offers a non-judgmental forum

---

[1]Peter Brook, "Or So The Story Goes," *Parabola*, 11 (2), (1986).

for the sharing of personal stories.

Secondly, the microcosm of a Playback Theatre performance (or other event) is a benign one. Respect is a cornerstone. No one is exploited or ridiculed or demeaned. It is safe, even nurturing. This atmosphere alone is enough to engender healing. People who experience it for any length of time—company members, or groups that use Playback in regular meetings, or participants in a workshop that lasts a few days—may grow simply from being in such an environment of acceptance and generosity.

The other essential element in Playback's healing effect is aesthetic. Stories are not just told, they are responded to with the artistic sensibility of the Playback team and shaped into pieces of theatre. Aesthetic choices are made. The ritual aspects we looked at in chapter 7 serve as a frame to enhance the form within.

What is happening in the artistic process, when life is distilled into art, in Playback or any other medium? The artist is someone who, like the visionary or the dreamer, senses the pattern that connects the disparate phenomena of our existence. She creates a form, in space or time or both, that in some way expresses her perception of this underlying coherence, or some piece of it. This is the root of the artistic process—the sensing of meaning and its depiction in form. The pleasure that the perceiver feels when he or she experiences the artist's creation also comes from the search for meaning. We fear chaos and meaninglessness, and too often experience them. When we encounter something that reflects our own experience in aesthetic form, we are reassured, even inspired. The degree to which this happens depends on how much we see our experience reflected in the artist's work and how much courage, depth, and conviction the artist has been able to summon.

In Playback Theatre, we are saying that by letting

ourselves *be* artists, we can reveal the pattern and beauty latent in the raw material of a life. Our aesthetic attention allows the story to become a testament to an ontological meaning and purpose. The aesthetic dimension—meaning an integrity of form, not necessarily harmonious or pretty—is itself a fundamental and profoundly affirming agent of healing.[2]

Pierre tells a story about how he was kidnapped as an infant by his maternal grandparents, who wanted to break up his parents' marriage. His manner gives no clue to his feelings about this extraordinary event. The conductor asks him to focus on the moment he wants to see. He chooses the courtroom scene where his grandparents are punished by being deported back to Europe. The actor playing the judge takes some creative liberties with her role. She becomes the furious avenger. "How dare you do such a thing?" she screams, stalking from her judge's bench and towering over the defendants in her flowing judicial robes. "You have no right to destroy this family. Don't you know how terrified they all were, including this little child?" On one side of the stage is an actor playing Pierre at fifteen, watching this scene from his own past in the sheltering company of an aunt.

When it's over, Pierre quickly resumes his flippant style of interaction with the conductor, but not before we have seen how engaged he was by the scene. He tells us that he may soon go to Europe and meet his grandparents for the first time since he was a baby.

At a workshop, Laine, a young single woman, comes to the teller's chair without a story clearly in mind. She feels she is

[2]See J. Salas, "Aesthetic Experience in Music Therapy," *Music Therapy*, 9, 1, (1990): 1-15.

at a crossroads in her life, and wants to explore her options for the future. The conductor encourages her to imagine a moment from her life a few years from now. Gradually, as Laine's creativity responds to the conductor's intuitive questioning, a vivid picture emerges. She sees herself as a performer, famous and successful, ending a performance that has been both touching and funny. Then she goes home to her family.

"How many children do you have?" asks the conductor.

"Four," says Laine without hesitation. She gives them all names and ages.

"And what's a word for your husband?"

"Loving. And playful."

When the scene is acted out, Laine wipes tears from shining eyes.

"Oh, I hope so! I hope so!" she says.

Both of these tellers took the risk of exposing their vulnerability on the Playback stage. Their sense of benefits that might be found drew them to tell their stories. What was it they gained? For Pierre, the value may have been mostly in bearing public witness to his experience. There was something almost defiant in his rather obstructive interactions with the conductor during the interview, perhaps in protection of his feelings about such a shameful episode in his family. But he found that his story was met with a compassionate respect from actors and audience alike. In response, his sarcasm was softened at the end of the scene. It is also likely that Pierre benefitted from simply seeing this moment enacted in flesh and blood right in front of him, instead of in his mind's eye, where undoubtedly it had played over and over again all his life. The mastery he gained by seeing this painful memory so fully externalized will probably stand him in good stead when he confronts his grandparents for the first time as an adult.

For Laine, who told her story in the supportive intimacy of a workshop, there was a conscious invoking of this group's collective creativity, manifested not only in the actual enactment, but also in the general atmosphere of rich imaginative possibility. It was her own vision, but she could not have brought it to life alone; nor perhaps could she even have flown freely enough in her own imagination to find the scenario that fulfilled her still-forming needs and desires.

Many people, seeing or hearing about Playback Theatre, ask "So is it theatre or is it therapy?" They see someone like Laine reaching for the Kleenex, they see people telling about pain and loss, they see performers who appear to be much more caring than one might expect theatre people to be, and neither remote nor glamorous, though they may be very talented. Some audience members may feel confused by Playback's gestalt that seems to include elements that they are used to thinking of as separate. The fact is that the values and practices of Playback Theatre do not conform to the functional divisions that are customary in modern society. Healing and art are *both* integrally part of Playback's purpose.

Playback practitioners have learned to live with this ambiguity and the effects of it in the world. As well as the daily challenge of explaining Playback Theatre to people, sometimes having to justify our work to sceptical friends and relatives, there have been some very pragmatic consequences. For many of us, it has meant that recognition, including in the form of grant support, has been hard to come by. Arts councils tend to say, "You're too therapeutic, you're obviously not totally committed to theatre." Social service funding sources often mistrust the degree to which we *are* seriously artistic. Ironically, it seems that this Catch-22 happens less to the newer groups, because they now have almost two decades of Playback Theatre tradition to point to.

Playback in Therapy[3]

Many of the people now trained in Playback Theatre come from the helping professions. (Some are drama therapists and psychodramatists, already familiar with the therapeutic effectiveness of using drama to explore personal experience.) Increasingly, they have begun to make use of Playback's healing qualities in their work in hospitals, clinics, residential and day treatment, and private practice. The ways in which this ritualized story-telling is broadly therapeutic to the general public also make it a valuable tool with children and adults who suffer from emotional difficulties and mental illness. People in treatment have a pressing need to tell their stories, and are likely to have less opportunity to do so than the rest of us.

Mental health professionals, encountering Playback for the first time, often express concern about the dangers of "opening people up" by inviting them to tell their stories. As they become more familiar with the form, they see that several factors serve to protect against the kind of loss of boundary that they are picturing. One is the skills of the therapist-conductor, who is trained to guide the telling of the story with clinical sensitivity. Another is the distancing effect of the form itself—there is a built-in control when the teller watches but does not participate in the drama. And thirdly, almost all tellers, whether they are psychiatric patients or members of the public, follow an innate sense of what is

---

[3]Techniques and issues of Playback Theatre in therapy warrant a much more detailed discussion than I am offering in these pages. The following comments may provide stimulus and further thought, but are not intended to be a guide to clinical practice, which needs to be well supported by clinical skills and experience.

See also "Playback Theatre: Children Find Their Stories" in *Handbook for Treatment of Attachment-Trauma Problems in Children*, Beverly James (New York: Lexington Books, 1994); and the *Interplay* issue on Playback Theatre and therapy, Vol. 5, 3.

appropriate to tell in any particular context. I've seldom seen this violated, even though no directives are given as to what may be told. Playback tellers instinctively gauge what level of self-disclosure is safe for them, depending on factors such as the size of the group and who else is present.

The sharing of stories takes place in an atmosphere that is not only safe but fundamentally benign and loving as well. It is a therapeutic environment that somewhat resembles the "unconditional positive regard" of Carl Rogers' person-centered therapy (an approach that is much more common, unfortunately, in private therapy than in treatment centers). And the aesthetic dimension is as profoundly healing for disturbed patients as it is for anyone else, possibly more so. Many troubled people are acutely in need of any experience that can hint at the existence of an underlying pattern that might make some sense of their suffering. Beauty of any kind tends to be in short supply in the lives of our most troubled fellow beings, and they are the ones who need it the most. Equally, they need opportunities to experience their own creativity, imagination, and spontaneity. It can be from such experiences that the sense of authorship of their own lives begins to grow, leading to increased autonomy and health.

At a home for severely emotionally disturbed children, ten children, boys and girls, aged between seven and ten, have come to the gym for a Playback Theatre show. Most of them have seen Playback before, several times. The performers are staff members—recreation workers, expressive arts therapists, a teacher, a psychologist—who give regular performances for children and staff. The second story is told by Cosmo. I choose him because he was so crushingly disappointed not to be chosen for the first story, and has already complained that he didn't get to tell in the last show either.

As he responds to my first few questions, Cosmo's story

117

veers dizzyingly around a number of different topics. His hold on reality seems rather tenuous, which happens sometimes with these children as they struggle through the ongoing traumas of their lives. I help him focus by asking him who he wants to see in his story, since "what" and "where" and "when" are not getting us anywhere. His mother, he says. A sad scenario begins to emerge. Cosmo is with his foster-parents. They don't under-stand how upset and worried he is about his mother, who is in jail for drug-related crimes.

The actors, most of whom know him well, construct a scene out of the elements that Cosmo has given us. It builds up to a poignant conversation between Cosmo and his mother. Karen, playing the mother, speaks from behind a jail made of milk-crates, while the teller's actor lies in his bed. It's as if they're in some realm of the heart where they can talk like this. The mother tells him how sad and sorry she is. She says that she hopes things will get better, but she just doesn't know. Her son listens and tells her how he loves her, and how he worries about her. It's the best they can do. There are no easy answers or happy endings.

Cosmo is very absorbed by the scene. So are most of the other children. He's not the only one whose life has been torn apart by an addicted parent. A couple of the children ease their tension by giggling a little. "It's not funny," scowls Cosmo. "They know it's not funny," I whisper to him. "Just watch the story."

After one more scene, we end the show with some quiet art work, the children spreading out on the floor of the gym with their childcare workers and members of the Playback team. It's a way to help the them find closure before returning to their living unit. Cosmo draws a huge heart with bars across it, with his mother looking out of a tiny window in the middle.

What were the therapeutic gains for Cosmo in this

experience? First of all, it meant a great deal to him to have this chance to tell his story. In spite of his initial confusion, the story that soon emerged was his deepest, most important story, the one that he lives with night and day, that underlies all the other events in his life. He had a strong drive to tell this, to share it in front of his peers and his staff, to identify himself in these terms both for his own sense of self and because he wanted others to understand this about him.

It was very important that his story was told in an atmosphere of acceptance. At these Playback shows, we always emphasize the importance of listening in a friendly, respectful way. Our own attentive response to every teller helps to provide a model. To a surprising degree, considering these children's pressing problems and the climate of harsh-ness that tends to prevail here, they are in fact able to hear each other's stories and watch the enactments with a generally sympathetic attentiveness. It takes frequent reminders on my part, but they seem able to suspend, to some degree, their usual ungenerous interactions. So Cosmo felt safe enough to risk this most vulnerable of stories, knowing the Playback format would create a secure enough context.

Children have often told similarly self-disclosing stories in our shows. I believe that part of what makes it safe for them is also the fact that their stories are simply told and enacted. We do not analyze or discuss them, although we may bring some of our knowledge of the child into the way the scene is carried out. In Cosmo's scene, Karen, the actor playing his mother, knew that there is little hope for this woman to become anything like the mother that Cosmo needs and deserves. Whatever Cosmo's dreams of reunion and fulfillment with her may be, her pattern so far makes it unlikely that she will free herself from the destructive cycle of addiction, crime, and imprisonment. Karen's awareness of this informed her acting. Her words in the scene eloquently expressed the mother's love and remorse, while carefully avoiding any overly optimistic messages. She found a way to communicate that whatever happened, she would think of him and love him. That was the extent of Karen's interpretation—an attempt, staying within the form, to provide a message that would be healing to Cosmo.

As his story was told and enacted, it was transformed from being a confused wash of painful thoughts, feelings, and images to being a theatrical piece endowed with the actors' creative artistry. Their aesthetic sense of story, in conjunction with their compassion and understanding, enabled them to find a coherent, satisfying form for Cosmo's experience. Art, as I said earlier, distills life into forms that convey some sense of pattern and purpose. The facts of Cosmo's life of course could not be changed by telling a story. But his pain could, to some degree, be redeemed by the experience of seeing it transmuted into something organized and artistically rendered. The presence of *art* was an essential aspect of the healing.

In a psychiatric hospital, there is a new patient who is making everybody nervous. He's big and loud and carries with him the Vietnam vet's aura of bitter wisdom. He is assigned to a psychodrama group.[4] Judy, the leader, is also an experienced Playback practitioner.[5] One day, Adam's struggles become the focus of the session. He's not willing to become the protago-

---

[4]Psychodrama differs from Playback Theatre in its problem-oriented focus, the length of the drama—often an hour or more—and the fact that the teller, called the "protagonist," acts in his or her own drama. For a discussion of the differences and affinities between the two methods, see J. Fox's article "Die inseszenierte personlische Geschichte im Playback-Theater" (Dramatized Personal Story in Playback Theatre) in *Psychodrama: Zeitschrift fur Theorie und Praxis,* June, 1991.

[5]Judy Swallow, a founding member of the original company, and director of Community Playback Theatre.

nist in a psychodrama. Judy, sensing the other group members'
desire to find a way to help, invites him to tell a story, Playback-
style. The other patients will act it out. He can just watch.

Adam tells about growing up in a family where feelings
were not acknowledged and not expressed. One day, the old
family dog becomes very sick. Hiding his worry from his parents,
Adam goes to bed when he's told, but later sneaks back down-
stairs to lie down with the dog, giving comfort and receiving it
too.

When he watches the scene, Adam weeps. His tears last
a long time. Later he tells everyone that he hasn't been able to
cry for years.

In the following days on the ward, Adam begins to initiate intimacy with several of the most fragile women patients.
Some of the staff are concerned about the women, and angry
at Adam for jeopardizing their stability. Judy wonders if Adam
is seeking ways to experience his tenderness, as he did with the
dog. Although she doesn't discuss her thoughts with Adam, she
feels he may have made some similar connections when he tells
her, at his discharge, that he has a lot to think about.

Meanwhile, some of the issues raised by Adam's story
have continued to develop for other members of the group.
One of the women to whom he paid his romantic attentions
says in a group session that she is beginning to realize that she
may have a habit of playing the sickly victim—being a pathetic,
needy creature, like Adam's dog. She was not actually present
when he told his story, and yet the learning and insight that
it embodied have become part of the group's collective story.
Another development is the opening up of the sensitive issue
of race. Adam, who is white, chose a black patient to be his
beloved dog, and another white patient to be himself. In the
enactment, the teller's actor is at first embarrassed by his task
of expressing tenderness, perhaps especially with a black fellow
actor. But Adam's emotion as he watches the scene lifts the

teller's actor from his inhibitions, and he is able to put a great deal of conviction into his acting. The group sees these two men, one black, one white, in an embrace of compassion. This image endures beyond Adam's story to become a human, positive point of departure for the exploration of racial themes, a potentially fraught area which had been hovering in the group's unspoken agenda for some time.

Often, so far, it has been psychodramatists who have seen Playback Theatre's potential as a clinical tool. It has been used as a warm-up, enacting stories Playback-style with patients who are not ready to launch into a full-fledged psychodrama. Sometimes, Playback may be used in place of psychodrama, perhaps with a protagonist who is too vulnerable to be in the thick of her story, who can gain much more from the distance provided by the teller's chair. In private therapy, individual clients, families, or couples have been able to view their lives and interactions in new, creative ways, leading to insight and change. In addictions treatment, Playback Theatre has provided a non-judgmental, non-threatening forum in which clients may find the courage to look at themselves with honesty.

Practical Options

There are a variety of ways that Playback Theatre can be brought into clinical settings, depending on client needs, staff availability, funding, and other factors. Here are some possibilities:

The work may be led by a clinician working alone, or at least without other Playback-trained staff on hand (although willing staff members can provide very helpful support even if they are new to Playback). Sometimes, as with Adam's story, the other patients in a therapy group are high-functioning enough to be actors in each other's stories. In this case, the healing benefits extend to the actors as well as to the teller. It is extremely therapeutic for a patient to realize that she can help by taking on a role in someone else's story. Suddenly, she is someone with gifts to give, no longer defined only by her deficits. The creativity that psychiatric patients may access as they fulfill a story will also promote their own growth. And, as we saw, one person's story may embody themes of importance for others, or for the group as a whole.

Therapeutic Playback sessions may take place when a company is contracted to come into a facility for a single event or for a series of ongoing shows. At a residential treatment center that rehabilitates sex offenders and addicts among the clergy, the treatment plan includes regular performances by the local Playback Theatre company. In shows like these, most of the acting is done by the company members, perhaps with the patients or clients taking on roles in some of the scenes.

To offer Playback to clients who are not able to be actors themselves, you may be able to set up an in-house group made up of permanent staff of the institution or agency. The group that enacted Cosmo's story is an in-house group. They attend regular lunchtime rehearsals to learn Playback Theatre, and they perform for groups of children about once a month. One of the advantages of a group like this is that they are familiar with the culture and events of the institution, and with the children themselves. This familiarity greatly enriches their work. The children love to be invited to participate in the scenes, as well as to tell stories. But they are not ready to be full-fledged Playback actors, at least in the context of a performance. For these children to succeed in taking on another's role, they would need considerably more structure and supervision than a performance mode allows.

Issues and Adaptations

Practicing Playback Theatre with groups of mental health patients, it becomes especially important to take great care with group process and sociometry—the art of attending to the constantly shifting balance of allegiances, identities, and concerns that are part of any group. The success of Playback depends on the group dynamics: even with emotionally wounded people it is possible and necessary to ensure that stories are chosen, told, and enacted in ways that promote trust and respect.

Offering Playback in clinical settings will probably call for some creative adaptations of the form, according to both the patients' needs and the overall situation. For example, the pace may be slowed down so that the conductor is sure that each element of the story fits precisely (though not necessarily literally—there's a difference) with the teller's subjective experience. In another adaptation, the conductor experiments with the physical placement of the scene, seeking to find the distance from the action that will allow the teller maximum involvement without overwhelming him. As the conductor, you may ask the teller to step into the scene at strategic moments, creating a blend of Playback and psychodrama. You might stay with one teller and do a series of scenes, each one building from the one before. Some Playback forms may work in a particular situation while others don't. The group that performs for disturbed children has found that pairs are too abstract for these children to readily comprehend, and so we tend not to include pairs in our shows. Others may notice an especially lively response to fluid sculptures and end up using them as much or more than full-length scenes. Playback may lend itself to a new kind of conflict resolution where the quarreling group members each tell their stories, then watch the other one's story. Something about the full, non-judgmental attention given to each story, and the sequential juxtaposition rather than simultaneous confrontation, seems to create a climate in which the adversaries can loosen their fierce hold on their positions because they feel so fully heard. Playback can be used for problem-solving, along the lines of Boal's Forum Theatre and other models in which audience members are invited to suggest more adaptive outcomes for the teller's story.

The Importance of Liaison

The safety and effectiveness of what may go on in a Playback Theatre therapy group depends to some degree on what kind of continuity and liaison may exist with other clinical staff. Do they understand and support what is happening? Are there ways that events in the Playback group can be followed up by other staff if necessary? Part of the work may be educating the rest of the staff, both clinical and direct care workers, about Playback, perhaps by creating opportunities for them to experience it for themselves.

This is another situation where the conductor also needs to fulfill the role of organizer and diplomat. Hard as it may be in some circumstances—either because of a lack of receptiveness, or simply time constraints—it is essential to create an atmosphere in which it is as safe and therapeutic as possible for the patients to reveal their stories. What happens in a Playback group or performance must be integrated with the other aspects of their treatment.

The Therapist as Artist

At an outpatient clinic where a Playback-trained therapist runs a weekly group for eight adult patients, Janice is telling a story.

"This happened on the way here this morning. I got off the bus and right at the edge of the hospital grounds I saw a little bird that looked like it couldn't fly." The conductor, Dan, interrupts her gently.

"Janice, who's going to be you in the story?"

She looks at the others. *"Sue, I guess."*

"And what's a word for how you were feeling?"

Janice grins at him. She knows this is not a casual question. *"Good! I'm doing good."*

He asks her to pick someone to play the bird. She chooses Damon. *"Helpless"* is her word for the bird. She goes on. *"So anyway, I stood there and looked at the poor little thing and wondered what I should do. I didn't like just leaving it there. I mean, it was so close to the road. I could just see it hopping in front of a car and smash, bye bye birdie."* She flutters her fingers and laughs nervously. *"But if I picked it up, maybe the other birds would smell my hands on it and peck it to death. That's what I thought. So that's it."*

"What happens in the end, Janice?"

"I just left it there and came here."

The story is acted out. When it is over, Dan tells the actors to stay in position, and keeps Janice in the teller's chair.

"Janice, look at yourself over there. Look at the little bird. What does it remind you of?"

Janice looks. *"Um, I guess that bird is a bit like me."*

Dan nods encouragingly. *"Who was it who walked away when you were little and helpless and wounded, Janice?"*

She hesitates. *"My mother, I suppose."*

With Dan's questions, a new story emerges, or rather an old story, the story of Janice's betrayal by her mother in her early childhood. This story is enacted too. Janice is moved, and so are some of the others. A long discussion follows, about old wounds, and danger, and helping or not helping, being supported or being abandoned.

In this vignette, the therapist-conductor is using the story as a way of approaching Janice's early, traumatic childhood experience. This psychodynamic, analytical use of personal story can be very effective—as we can see above, a here-and-now event may well contain echoes of other, perhaps more painful experiences in the teller's life. The Playback process can be used to make these echoes explicit, to bring the unconscious into the conscious, which Freud said was the goal of psychotherapy.

But, therapeutic as this kind of work may be, Playback's healing power may actually be undercut by such adaptations. Something is lost.

The meaning of a personal story is often held in a suspension of layers. Imagine a chord that is spread from one end of the keyboard to the other. You may sense the deepest bass note that resonates almost below hearing. And yet if you strip away all the harmonies and dissonances that float above it, the exposed fundamental tone will be weakened. As in this musical chord, the meaning of a Playback story lies somewhere in the dynamic, resonant relationship between all the elements and in the echoes connecting the layers of allusion.

In our example, Dan, the conductor, led Janice's story firmly in the direction of one particular facet of its meaning. He was working according to the psychodynamic principle which considers that significant present experience always has some relation to early childhood, usually to early childhood trauma. True as this may be, it seems to me that this aspect of the meaning does not have to be isolated in order for the patient to learn and grow from it. In fact, the story's greatest power and effect will probably lie in its multiplicity of related meanings. Dan's treatment of the story may have actually diminished its healing effect for Janice.

What is lost in such a moment is the healing that can

be brought specifically through art, which works through allusion and metaphor, through the call to imagination, intuition, and creativity, and the acknowledgment of beauty. If Janice's story had been fully honored as she told it, she—and the other group members—would have been left with a richly suggestive image whose meanings might have emerged differently for each person. As the conductor, Dan could have enhanced the story's therapeutic effect without resorting to interpretation: for example, by encouraging the teller's actor to play the role with a full expressiveness; or by offering the possibility of a transformation. Perhaps, after seeing her experience portrayed as it happened, Janice would herself have been inspired to imagine a fulfillment of this moment that might have been healing for her, and the group, on all of its intricately interwoven levels.

One reason why Dan did not trust the story to stand alone may have been his own lack of ease in the domain of art, his own unfamiliarity with the role of artist. It may be the greatest challenge that clinicians have to deal with when they bring Playback into their work—how to bring what is among other things an art form into the world of clinical practice. Even though people like Dan may have experienced the powerful healing force of creativity and art and story for themselves in workshops and training sessions, they are more comfortable as clinicians than as artists. They may find themselves reluctant to trust the relatively uncharted realm of art once they are working with patients whose needs and fragility they are acutely, conscientiously aware of.

The healing power of aesthetic experience is still under-explored and incompletely comprehended. Like any new frontier, it may arouse mistrust, or at least cautiousness. But this may change, as the world of psychology becomes increasingly hospitable to approaches that value not only phenomenological experience but story itself, the "royal road to epistemology."[6]

Meanwhile, there are others who succeed in using the full, artistic Playback process in their therapeutic work. They have found that even with a group of psychiatric patients in a sterile hospital room, with no other Playback actors there to help out, you can invite the presence of art. You can communicate the importance of the ritual framework. You can transform the space with colorful props and a theatrical arrangement of chairs. Most of all, you can give your own inner artist the freedom to see and celebrate the poetry of the stories that are told, and you can invite the participants to find their own artistry as they bring each others' stories to life. You can trust in the fullness of the story to hold its many-layered meanings, and trust that the teller will receive the wisdom and insight of the group as it manifests in the scene, to the degree that he is ready to receive it.

Healing and Art Intertwined

Ironically, the growing and successful use of Playback Theatre in therapy makes it even harder to explain what Playback is, since many people may now encounter it first in a therapeutic context. "No, it's not primarily a therapeutic modality, though it can be used that way, no, you don't have to be a therapist to do it, yes, we do Playback in public theatres, with the general public, yes, even there we are concerned that it be a healing experience, in the broadest sense, for everyone, including the actors."

Wherever Playback Theatre takes place, and for whomever, it intertwines elements that are commonly separated in our culture, as so many things are separated. Naturally, different contexts may well call for an emphasis

---

[6]Bradford Keeney, *Aesthetics of Change*, (New York: Guilford Press, 1983), 195.

on either the art or the healing aspect, and some groups or individual practitioners may choose to specialize. A group that performs frequently in public theatres may pay special attention to artistic standards of performance and presentation. A therapist in a hospital will use sophisticated therapeutic knowledge that would not be necessary with ordinary audiences. But although the ratio of these elements may vary, they are both integral to Playback. Art and healing are both irreducibly part of this work.

9

Being in the Community

Some moments:

We are performing in a public theatre in New York. We are nervous about the "theatre-ness" of it; it's a more formal setting than we are used to. There is a stage and black curtains and good publicity. Audiences are used to seeing plays here— what will they make of our theatre of personal improvisation? When the show begins, it's clear that this is very different from our public performances at home. These are New Yorkers, strangers to each other, strangers even to the idea of com- munity. We feel their attitude of "Show me!" and we wonder if we can. We keep to our form, and the stories come. Slowly, some connection grows, between us and them, between each other. But we leave feeling it hasn't happened quite enough. We have not really succeeded in transforming this sophisticated group into the "audience of neighbors" on which Playback's success depends.

Another New York City performance. This time we're in a high school in a poor neighborhood. We fall silent as the front doors are unlocked for us by an armed security guard. We are told that a student was shot to death on these steps the first day of the semester. There are about thirty kids waiting for us in the classroom where we have been invited. They're all black. We're all white. It's only the trust and respect they have for their teacher which save us from being laughed out the door before we even start. Once we get going, their hunger to be heard begins to outweigh their suspiciousness. We invite them to help act out the stories. There's a lot of self-conscious giggling, but they do it. Their stories tell of the fears and dangers that surround them: these children live in a war zone and neither teachers nor parents nor the law can keep them safe. When we end, one boy lingers as we pack up. He talks about his own survival strategies. We're struck by his philosophical good humor; wisdom, perhaps.

We are at a family therapists' conference being held at a college empty for the summer. Our performance has been scheduled to take place in a gym-size multi-purpose room, chilly with air-conditioning. Straight rows of folding chairs are dwarfed by the high ceiling and vast shiny floor. Before we begin, we ask the therapists to help us rearrange their chairs in curving rows so that they can see each other. Within the circle created by the audience and our own stage set-up, we do our best to foster the connection and affirmation that they are seeking together. They tell stories about mysterious and frustrating and triumphant times in their therapy sessions—and their personal lives. At the end of the show the room feels warmer.

The social worker at the local county jail arranges a performance. We file in past beefy men bulging with weapons and keys. My bag of instruments is searched by a guard, each tambourine and guiro held up for inspection. He looks at them and sees weapons, not music. "You can't take this, or this, or this." The prisoners are gathered in a windowless cafeteria that smells of disinfectant. They seem genial and pleased to see us. Their stories are about how they got set up, how their girlfriends have left them, what it's going to be like getting out. Afterwards, they cluster around us, longing for contact. Most of all, they want to keep telling their stories. Some of them will get a chance to: one of our actors is coming back to do a series of workshops with them.

We're in a dance studio in our home town. There are graceful arching windows looking down onto the street, and wide polished floorboards. The room is full of parents and children. We know many of them, and they know us. The stories flow one after another. A mother tells a childhood memory that her own children have never heard before. A little boy picks his father to act in his story about a nightmare. There's a rush of injury stories told by the four to seven-year-olds, preoccupied with the mastery of their physical world. The conductor tries to redirect them, just for variety. "I see some grandparents with us here today. Who'd like to tell a story about a special time with your grandma or grandpa?" Three hands go up. "Yes, Jacob?" "I fell down the back steps and I got stitches."

These are all vignettes from performances with the original company. Most Playback groups could relate a similarly broad sampling of performing experiences. Bringing our story forum into all these corners of the community, including some where theatre is not usually seen, is our bread and butter—not always our remuneration, but our substance, our daily fare.

Creating a Space for Playback

For most of the shows mentioned above, we came to do our work in a space that was customarily used for some purpose other than performance. In some cases, like the jail, the room was outright inhospitable what we were there to do. Of all these contexts, only the last, the family show in the dance studio, was fully welcoming to Playback Theatre. The space was intimate, aesthetic, full of signs of creative activity. The audience already felt connected to Playback Theatre and to each other.

When Playback events are not like this, and most of them aren't, our first task is to do whatever is possible to transform the space. In part this is simply logistical—we need a certain amount of room to move, etc. But it is more than that; arranging the room is part of the ritual of performance, as we saw in chapter 7.

The less hospitable the atmosphere, the more you have to prepare not only the space but the audience—explain, reassure, model the process. And you have to be patient. People for whom the idea of public self-disclosure is new and alarming may take a whole show to get to a level of openness that another group may have at the outset. This is true in workshop as well as performance situations. One of the hardest Playback experiences we ever had was with a group of adolescents in a maximum security prison. They had all been convicted of felonies, including murder, rape, and armed robbery. Four of us from the original company worked with them for a series of ten sessions. It took about seven of these sessions for the inmates to be willing to sit in a circle. Each week there was a tiny movement toward trust. In the beginning they tried to shock and disgust us with stories of violence and depersonalized sex, drawn more from slash movies than from their own lives—not that their lives lacked such experience, but they were not ready to expose themselves by telling their truth. By the end, they gave us some unexpected glimpses of vulnerability, even tenderness. One of the final stories was about raising pigeons on the roof of a New York City tenement, proudly watching them fly away, anxiously waiting for their return, wondering how they were doing now.

Playback Theatre and Idealism

Why do we do Playback in settings that are so difficult, either in terms of the physical space, or the group's attitude, or both?

From the beginning, this theatre was conceived as a theatre of gift. It was to be offered to the world as a means of healing interaction, as I discussed in the last chapter. We knew that everyone has stories and the need to tell them, however reserved they might appear. We were committed to bringing this forum to the "unstoried" as well as to those who already knew the satisfaction of sharing stories. As we tried to fulfill this ideal in our first years, the rewards and successes repeatedly (though sometimes just barely) outweighed the frustrations and obstacles. On the whole, it felt wonderful to do theatre for people who would never go to see a play, who would think that such cultural experiences were meant for other people entirely. Seeing the look on the face of a teen-age mother as she realized that these adults really did want to hear and honor her story could make up for the ugly, noisy room and the forty-five minutes of awkward reaching for a common language.

We began in the mid-seventies, a time when the world-changing sixties still influenced the current consciousness. Our desire to be a force for social healing and change was not inconsistent with the spirit of the times. By the selfish Reagan eighties, we were out of step. It was a challenge to our group self-esteem to continue to feel strong about Playback's social role. One young man, when I explained to him that Playback was a non-profit corporation, said: "Soon to be a profit-making corporation, right?" He didn't understand the validity of working for ideals rather than profit.

Not that we didn't also try hard to earn money. We applied for grants, and sometimes got them—almost always for work in the social service area. Our artistic explorations continued, with great energy and often aesthetic success, but little recognition from arts councils. So we ran our company on grants like the one that had us using Playback Theatre to teach retarded people how to use public transport—work that was certainly a test for our humility. But even this sometimes brought delights. I'll never forget the little couple, middle-aged but innocent as nine year-olds, sitting hand-in-hand in their group home, and beaming as they told about their first unescorted trip on the rural bus.

This practice of offering Playback to the disenfranchised has remained an important feature for many, probably most Playback Theatre companies. It is a characteristic that distinguishes Playback Theatre from other recent redis-coveries of the importance of personal story. I'm thinking particularly of the loosely-defined field of contemporary or personal mythology whose leading figures include Joseph Campbell and Robert Bly. Significant and influential as their work may be, it is helpful mainly to those who read books on mythology, who consult Jungian therapists, who attend workshops at growth centers, who travel to conferences at big hotels. In contrast, Playback Theatre's earthy simplicity and directness make it readily accessible to almost anyone. The work can have immediate relevance to people of all levels of education, sophistication, and means. A homeless woman in Washington, DC may never join the local Playback company, but they may come and perform at her shelter, and she may tell her story.

Playback in the Private Sector

Not all Playback groups have stayed with this traditional emphasis on social service work. At the other end of the spectrum, with its own kind of idealism, is the work that is being done in organizational development with private business. Since about 1989, a number of Playback groups and individual practitioners have found ways to bring their work into this arena. Here, Playback Theatre can be a forum in which truths are told, experiences validated, old management practices challenged and re-visioned, all in a constructive, creative way.

In a work environment that is rigidly hierarchical, as many are, those whose task is to carry out the decisions of others may lack much sense of accomplishment or satisfaction or connection in relation to their work—a serious loss, when you think of the amount of time that most people spend at their jobs. In some businesses, upper level management seems to be realizing at last that their own goals of increased productivity are likely to be served if the line workers can feel more invested and rewarded by their work. These managers are ready to explore new ideas, like Playback, that may engender alternatives to stale structures and stagnant communications.

What actually happens when workers are invited to tell their stories may be more than the CEOs imagined. Emotions may be stirred up, shared, listened to; pride and truth may show themselves in places where they've never been seen before. A man cries publicly for the first time in his life and says, "I never believed that emotions were worth much." Someone else says, "This restores my hope."

For the Playback group doing this work, there are both gains and dangers. There is the satisfaction of finding that one's work can reach and help yet another segment of the population. There is the revelation, for some, that people in striped ties or dress-for-success shoulder pads are still just people with stories to tell, no less human or fascinating than criminals, teachers, or artists. There is also the fact that so far this arena is the only one in which Playback people have the chance to earn significant amounts of money. Since work in other areas—either artistic performance or social services—seldom if ever pays enough to live on, it can be extremely gratifying—heady, even—to have a chance to be so well-rewarded for practicing your craft.

But there are costs, too. The prospect of large sums of money may lead to extreme pressures, especially if the movement in this direction is abrupt. Several of the groups specializing in private sector work have split up over issues of competitiveness and standards of presentation. Some members speak of the deep and unresolved pain of their struggles. Another loss, too, is the energy and time to go on performing for Playback's traditional constituencies.

Hearing about this pattern, I wonder if there is a two-way process at work. Perhaps, while they model and teach the humanizing values of Playback Theatre, these groups are also absorbing some of the not-so-generous values of the capitalist marketplace, and find themselves bruised by them.

Professionalism, Ambition, and Love

Whether or not a Playback group becomes involved in private sector work, it will sooner or later face the question of worldliness and its implications.

In the uncomplicated enthusiasm of starting a company, membership may be offered gratefully to anyone who's interested, without worrying too much about skill or experience. Then, as the work develops, so does a desire to reach for Playback's artistic potential. There's excitement and pride and the urge to share—"Let's take this out into the world!" The question of standards may begin to raise itself: are we good enough to perform? To ask for money at the door? To offer ourselves as a professional resource? Looking self-critically at artistic standards can lead to stress within the group if everyone does not share similar skill levels or a similar commitment to developing them. When the time comes to invite new people to join the company, there's likely to be a selection process: actors are sought who have the kinds of talents and capacities that the rest of the group has by now acquired. But some of the original members may privately wonder if they'd be accepted if they were auditioning.

The company continues to rehearse and perform and develop. Some of them love it so much that they want to use Playback as a way to support themselves—they think to themselves, this could be a career, not just an avocation. They're inspired by the work that they hear other Playback groups are doing. They see how Playback could be used in their own local agencies and community events. Some members of the group start to work in institutions, schools, businesses—and they get paid. Others have fulltime jobs that don't permit them to take part. For some companies, the division becomes a problem. The ambitious members feel held back by the others. They sense their own skills growing, while the others move at a slower pace. The company finds itself steering a tricky path around issues of professionalism, money, inclusiveness versus artistic excellence. Some groups run aground. Others are able to come to a place of consensus, perhaps deciding that the whole company is going to become professional, or perhaps simply accepting the range of skill levels and ambition and finding ways to accommodate it.

The most stable companies seem to find a balance between the demands and the attractions of artistic and professional fulfillment, on the one hand, and moving at a pace that allows for inclusiveness, on the other. This does mean letting go of the most vertiginous heights of ambition. You'll never be the toast of the talk shows or rate serious critical attention from the theatre world or earn large sums of money if you insist on being thoroughly true to the values of community—to "bringing each other forth" in Jean Vanier's definition. Instead, you are embracing the way of the citizen actor, one who works for love above all.

Playback in Education

Around the world, many groups and individual practitioners have explored the possibilities of Playback Theatre in education.[1] They have experimented with work in schools at all levels, and although some have been discouraged by school culture and conditions, others have succeeded, with diplomacy and persistence, in building a hospitable environment for Playback. Projects range from one-time performances to commitments that may extend over days or weeks, perhaps providing a forum for an issue that the school community is dealing with, or offering a novel way to explore curriculum material. Playback can even become a permanent feature—I know of two highly successful school-based companies, one in Alaska and one in New Hampshire. One is made up of high school students, identified as "at risk"—of suicide, alcoholism, and other dangers of the mine fields of adolescence—and the other of eleven and twelve-year-olds, who go out into the community performing at nursing homes and elementary schools.

All of the benefits of experiencing Playback Theatre that we've talked about so far are relevant and available to children: the affirmation, the sense of comprehension and mastery, the revelation that others share your experience, the delicate building of identity. And there are further gains for the children who have become Playback performers themselves. For young people who may have special needs for emotional and social support, like the Alaskan teenagers, the chance to belong to such a group may literally be a lifesaver. These young people have the satisfaction not only of sharing their own stories in a safe, intimate, consistent environment, they also find great pride in bringing their

---

[1] See J. Fox, "Trends in PT for Education," *Interplay*, 3, 3 (1993).

skills to public audiences.

The Playback process may have a role to play in the central task of learning itself, especially in the context of some of the recent trends in education. According to Gardner's theory of multiple intelligences, there are several identifiable kinds of intelligence beyond the two—linguistic and logical-mathematical—that are usually emphasized in education.[2] Children whose main learning modes are kinesthetic or spatial or interpersonal may be better able to grasp new concepts when they are explored in acted-out stories. Cooperative learning, another current direction in schooling, focuses on the benefits of pooling skills instead of competing. Playback creates an immediately rewarding teamwork experience, where success depends upon bringing forth each other's strengths. (Playback's capacity to facilitate learning can also be of value in adult education— for example, Playback Theatre has been used in teaching language to adult students in Australia, Germany, England, and the Czech Republic.)

In spite of Playback Theatre's obvious appeal to children and its clear relevance to learning, it's sometimes had an uneasy welcome in schools. Playback promises to honor not the status quo and the approved version of reality, but personal experience. And schools, like most institutions, are generally not places that validate the subjective truth of either the individual or the group. Logistics can be challenging, too—often it is hard to carve out the right congenial space for a Playback event in a school. Assemblies take place in huge auditoriums with too many kids, classrooms are full of desks, skull-jarring bells rudely truncate the last story.

---

[2] Howard Gardner, *Frames of Mind*, (New York: Basic Books, 1983).

Playback and Politics

There can be political reverberations to Playback Theatre's commitment to subjective truth. The message that your
story, my story, our stories have an unassailable validity is
radically empowering. In political contexts where the official
story does not acknowledge personal, subjective experience,
it is subversive. It is the telling and believing of real stories,
whispered, remembered, repeated, that can lead to the cry
for change, even for revolution. And after the revolution, it is
still the telling of the stories that keeps the truth from being
lost, co-opted by larger forces whether they are the new face
of oppression or the banal face of the media.

In 1991, we heard that a four-person film crew from
Soviet Central Television wanted to come to New Paltz to
film Playback Theatre at its source. They had already made
a film about the Moscow Playback Theatre company. They
wanted to add some footage of Jonathan to the beginning of
their film and shoot a new documentary about the original
company. A week before they were to arrive, the coup in
Moscow took the world by surprise. We were certain this
meant that the trip was off, and even more sure when, a
few days later, the coup was overthrown. Why would any
journalist want to leave Moscow in the middle of the story
of a lifetime? But they came, right on schedule.

Whatever other motivations might have been behind
their determination to get here—and it began to emerge
that a couple of them, at least, fondly imagined that filming
Playback Theatre might be a route to success in the world of
private enterprise—they came with a pressing need to tell their
stories about the events of the past week. They had been in
the thick of it. We set up an informal Playback performance.
Through an interpreter, Svetlana, the scriptwriter, told about
seeing a sobbing old woman throw herself onto a tank slowly

142

advancing towards the crowds on Gorky Street. "Kill me! Kill me!" she cried. "Don't kill them, they're young. Kill me, I've had my life!" The tank stopped, and a young soldier climbed out, himself in tears. Igor, the director, had been in the Russian parliament when Boris Yeltsin announced that the leaders of the coup were fleeing to the airport. Realizing this meant that the coup was over, Igor ran outside to tell the crowds of people. At first they didn't believe him. Then there was a great roar and singing and cheering. He also told about the funeral in Red Square of the three young men who were killed protesting the coup. The huge square was packed, he said, so many people that you couldn't move. But they were quiet, respectful, even gentle. When someone in the crowd fainted, people melted away as if by magic to allow an ambulance to come through.

Awed to see this turning point in history right in front of our eyes, we asked Svetlana why they had come at such a time. "Because what you do is about stories," she said, "and when have we ever needed our stories more than now?"

10

Growing in the World

The other day we got a letter from a new Playback group in Hungary. It was news to us that there was any Playback Theatre activity there. We haven't worked in that country and no-one from Hungary has yet come to our trainings here. We were delighted but not altogether surprised. By now we're used to the idea that Playback Theatre has its own independent life in the world, its own energetic and unpredictable patterns of growth.

It turns out that the people in Hungary had encountered Playback Theatre through a videotape of a Playback performance in Milan, led by a Swedish teacher of Playback who had trained here a number of years ago. There's always a chain of connections, if one wants to trace them. Playback Theatre's growth from the beginning has been person to person, group to group—a process that has meant a slow but organic and solid development. Over the years, most people have been drawn to Playback after seeing a show, or hearing friends talk about it. These days, there are increasing numbers of people who first meet Playback Theatre on the printed page. But if they are inspired to follow up this initial encounter, they find themselves in a network that is more like an oral tradition than anything else. Because our work is stories, it is through our stories that we know each other.

Years ago, when the possibility arose of others besides our original group doing Playback Theatre, we had to think about the questions of control and ownership and regulations. Some people advised us to register the name and franchise the process so we could make sure that anyone else practicing Playback Theatre was doing it in a way that was consistent with the practices and values we had established. In doing so, not only would we be able to monitor the standard of work done under the name of Playback Theatre, we would also stand to gain monetarily from the financial successes of other groups. This model was an accepted way of operating in the human potential movement as well as in business. But it never felt right for Playback Theatre. We leaned towards a different model, in which the idea is shared through face-to-face contact, not sold, and quality control is built into the process. Since Playback's effectiveness depends on the intrinsic quality of the work, anyone trying to practice Playback without due attention to respect, safety, and aesthetic grace is unlikely to succeed.

So we encouraged others to take our form and explore it, use it, play with it, share it. We made ourselves available for training and support. In 1990, we handed over our legal structure, including our tax-exempt status, to the new International Playback Theatre Network, formed to provide connection and support to Playback practitioners all over the world. We also decided that the time had come to get a service trademark for the name and logo of Playback Theatre. We recognized that as Playback moved into a level of activity we had never anticipated, it was prudent to have the capability of preventing the name from being misused. So far, such a need has not arisen. Networking and supportive feedback have kept the work faithful to its purpose and values. (See the Appendix for information on the IPTN and Playback's legal status.)

Cooperation and Competition

As Playback becomes more widespread, some groups are finding that they are not the only show in town. A company that has been active for six years may be disconcerted to hear that a new group is forming, drawing its members from a different network of people. Or perhaps this new group is an off-shoot of the old one, started by former members who may or may not be on good terms with the first group.

Such situations can be fraught with painful interactions and bad feeling on all sides. Territoriality raises its unattractive head; there are mutterings about ingratitude and upstarts and which group is better. But these transitions also offer the opportunity to put Playback's strengths to the test.

During the last few years of the original group's active life, we faced this kind of challenge when one of our members gathered some people together to do "living-room Playback"—meeting just for themselves, sharing stories, learning the form. After a while, naturally, their pleasure and sense of accomplishment demanded a forum more expansive than a living room, and they started to perform in the community—our community. Although by then we were winding down, it was difficult for us in many ways. One had to do with pride. Our area was associated with the original Playback group's work. When strangers came to performances by the new company, they often assumed that this was *the* Playback Theatre (even though the new group had a distinct name). At that stage, the new group had not developed skills that approached ours. It hurt to think that audiences would believe that it was our work that they were seeing. For the new company, the discrepancy in our respective levels of experience and renown were equally hard to take. As they struggled to draw people to their shows, we would without effort attract standing-room-only audiences to our very occasional performances.

But all along, both groups were committed to finding out how to coexist harmoniously. After all, we all believed in the values of inclusiveness and connection on which the work itself is based. So we looked for a new configuration, one that would encompass both our groups.

Over time, we've succeeded. The new group has become highly skilled and securely established. We sometimes attend each others' shows, and occasionally share the stage as guest performers. Although the two groups maintain their separate identities, we feel ourselves to be part of an extended Playback Theatre family, offering mutual support and sharing our resources. We even share equipment—the original group's lights and props, by now augmented and refurbished, are in constant use by the other group, and we borrow them back when needed.

There are companies in other places who have achieved a similar kind of cooperativeness; and there are others struggling with distance and competitiveness. For groups who are trying hard to support themselves, even partially, by doing Playback, the issue of money may add factors that are particularly sensitive. The prevailing economic viewpoint says that (a) there's a finite amount out there of what we want, and (b) the only way to get it is to be the successful competitor. It takes a larger vision to see that there's no limit to what Playback has to give, to whom, and in what contexts; and no limit to what may come back as recompense, in the form of money as well as other rewards.

Playback in Different Cultures

How is Playback Theatre different, or the same, in various places around the world? Let's look at three companies, one in New Zealand, one in France, and one on the west coast of the United States.

Playback Théâtre France is in Le Havre, a harbor city in the north of France with a strongly working-class identity. Like many French towns, they also have a sizable immigrant com-

munity. Most of them live on the plateau above the city. One, a man whose family came from Algeria a generation ago, is in the Playback company. Today he's assisting the leader at a Playback Theatre workshop. He has brought several friends from his community. They're people who have been creating their own theatre together. This is the first time they have experienced Playback. They're nervous. Most people in the workshop are European French, and they look as though they belong. In a beginning warm-up, the leader invites everyone to say something positive about themselves. The people from the plateau can't find things to say. They help each other. "She's a great cook!" "He's a very kind person." But there's no hesitation later, when it's time to tell stories. Here they share themselves freely, both as tellers and as actors. The other participants are impressed by their openness and their gifted acting. Seeing this, they're inspired themselves to go further, take more risks. The immigrant people also astonish everyone else with their lack of inhibition about music. There's no self-consciousness, no protests that they can't play well enough. Their music becomes a bridge. One man, who later joins the Playback group, emerges as a leader through his music. With his guitar and his songs, he brings everyone together. Preconceptions about each other that might have been there at the beginning are melted away, replaced by respect and rapport.

This Playback company began in the summer of 1988, following a workshop taught by Jonathan Fox. The founder and artistic director is Heather Robb (Bruyère in France), an Australian who came to France more than twenty years ago to study mime, mask, and clowning at the École Jacques Lecoq. She went on to become a teacher at Lecoq before moving to Le Havre where she now teaches in the municipally-supported École de Théâtre.

The company—eight to ten people—includes, like many

Playback groups, a wide range of vocational backgrounds, with a majority of people involved in the performing arts, teaching, and social work, and in some cases a combination of these. Their ages range from mid-twenties to late forties. The group's strengths are in their artistic sensibilities and experience—all have had theatre training at the École de Théâtre. They work hard to hone Playback Theatre as an aesthetic form.

During the winter months, Playback Théâtre France offers monthly public performances at a community arts center. They've also done public shows just for children, and for the constituents, sometimes from the poorest sections of the population, of other community centers. They're beginning to be seen as a resource for local industry, not for organizational development, but as a way to enrich special events for the workers and their families.

So far, this is a group of "citizen actors" who support themselves from their regular jobs and earn virtually nothing from their Playback performances, in spite of their seriousness and artistic sophistication. They are at the point in their development where the prospect, for the first time, of income-producing Playback work is leading to intense discussion about daytime availability, commitment, and ultimately, about their identity and goals as a group. It is a challenging transitional period: there is an overall interest in moving toward professionalism, but most of the actors do not have the kind of autonomy in their current employment that would readily allow them to explore the possibilities that may be there.

The Living Arts Theatre Lab in the San Francisco Bay area is another group for whom Playback has little if anything to do with earning a living. This group has reached a more relaxed stance on this issue than the French group, though.

They are choosing to do the work for its intrinsic satisfactions and do not plan to expand in the direction of finding income-producing work. Unlike the Le Havre group, several members of Living Arts are self-employed, or have a degree of flexibility in their jobs, so that accepting an occasional daytime offer does not have to entail difficult questions about career and commitment.

In other ways these groups have important characteristics in common. The Living Arts Theatre Lab is also firmly committed to work that is artistically fully realized; and to reaching out to people who are not usually part of a theatre-going audience. Like the French group, and like most other Playback groups, its fifteen members come from varied professional backgrounds. The worlds of therapy and the arts are well represented. The group's director, Armand Volkas, is a theatre director and actor who is also a drama therapist. Several others are also creative arts therapists of one kind or another, people whose professions lie in the conjunction of healing and art.

Living Arts offers the traditional Playback Theatre monthly public performance, held in a church hall. They also perform for senior citizens, for recovery groups, at a church service. They use Playback in a unique project that allows postwar-generation Jews and Germans to deal with the legacy of the Holocaust. Acts of Reconciliation, as it is called, was conceived by Armand, the son of European Jews who were resistance fighters in the Second World War until they were sent to concentration camps.

At a performance that is the culmination of a month-long process interweaving therapy and theatre, Wolf tells a story about his youth in Germany. He remembers being a child, perhaps five years old, playing with a group of boys. One of them teaches the others a song. Wolf is troubled by its images and harshness, though it's not until years later that he realizes that it is a Nazi marching song. At five, it's hard not to go along with the group. Pushing down his unease, he joins in with his friends as they march around singing at the tops of their voices.

There's a second part to this story. Wolf, now seventeen, is on vacation with his girlfriend in the south of France. They wander into a cemetery. Wolf finds himself in the Jewish section. He stands in front of a tomb that says: "In memory of Jews whose bodies were turned into soap." Staring at it, he hears the song.

Whether an Acts of Reconciliation performance or a show for the regular community, Living Arts sees the work as above all spiritual in nature. They are looking for contexts in which this dimension of Playback can best be fulfilled— maybe there's a church that would like to have a Playback company, the way churches often have choirs, says Armand. He's not entirely serious, but he's not unserious either.

In a steeply-raked lecture hall in New Zealand's capital city, Wellington Playback Theatre is performing for an audience of student nurses, young women and men, at the end of their first week of classes. It's one o'clock on a Friday afternoon: six members of the group are taking part in the performance, while others are busy with their regular jobs. Tonight they'll all get together for a training workshop.

The students are young, almost overwhelmed by their first week. They've never seen Playback before, and at first they are less than receptive. But with the conductor's skillful, patient questions, and the actors' expressive responses, the audience's trust and engagement grow. They begin to vent some of their feelings about the difficulties and even indignities of the week. They've all had to be immunized against contagious diseases, says one, angry about being subjected to the needle. The fluid sculpture that follows reflects her injured feelings. But in the middle of it one of the actors says, gleefully: "I'll do this to someone else one day." The students laugh in recognition.

As the show goes on, the theme changes. After the students have had plenty of chance to complain, the conductor slants her questions in another direction, inviting them to re-member what has led them to join this program. An instructor tells a story about a moment when, frustrated at being unable to communicate with an elderly Alzheimer's patient, she mas-sages the old woman's feet. The patient stops her incompre-hensible rambling and looks the nurse right in the eye. "That's lovely," she says. A young man remembers how moved he was at an orphanage in Manila. There was one child in particular, spirited in spite of a sadly distorted body. By the end of the show, the students have felt again the altruism and compassion that have brought them to nursing.

Wellington Playback Theatre has been active since 1987. Some of the members were also part of an earlier group that the director, Bev Hosking started after she took part in our first New Zealand workshop in 1980, before leaving to study improvisational theatre in Sydney. For Bev, it is most of all Playback's community aspect that draws her—both the community of the performing group itself and the role that the work can play in the community at large. The make-up of the group and the scope of their work reflect this interest. The fourteen members, mid-twenties to early forties, include professional actors, visual artists, a lawyer, a teacher of art and drama, a psychiatrist, training consultants, mothers, counsellors. They perform in schools, for church groups, in outlying small towns, for corporations and government departments, as well as for the general public in the local tramping club hall, decorated with topographical maps and a huge photo of Mount Ruapehu, a volcano that has never quite been tamed.

Wellington Playback Theatre is stable, consistently active, and very accomplished. They are committed to doing the work as well as they can, and to offering it as widely as they can. They balance these values with the reality that for all of them, their primary financial support comes from their other work, and leaves them limited amounts of time for Playback. Like many other groups, they can accept invitations to do daytime work if enough of the part-time or self-employed people are available. Some members are never free to do shows like the one for the nursing students. But so far the group has not been divided by this. These daytime performances are neither frequent nor lucrative enough to create subgroups of "professional" and "non-professional" members. Besides, reaching into the community is a mutually-held ideal, and the whole group can feel pleased about fulfilling it whether or not they are actually part of a particular performance.

Playback Theatre has been readily accepted in its New Zealand context. Their highly varied audiences seem to understand what Playback is there to do. The young nurses, many of them not more than eighteen years old and fresh from their small farming towns, were able to respond to the invitation to tell their stories, once they realized what was being asked of them. As in this show, the stories always come, even if slowly, and not especially inward-looking or emotionally dramatic. There is a cultural value on privacy, and audience members often need a good deal of encouragement getting to the teller's chair. What helps most of all is simply the example of the performers themselves, ordinary people standing up there, willing to try anything, willing to be seen. It's a kind of courage, and some audience members are inspired to discover it in themselves.

Connecting to the Surrounding Culture

Whatever the cultural climate, Playback Theatre is an innovative form that synthesizes elements that most people are used to experiencing separately, if at all. This means that every group must search for the place where their work can fit into their community and culture. If you were forming a repertory theatre or a group practice of therapists or a youth community center, you'd still have to go through the hard work of introducing yourselves and the project to the people you hope to attract. You'd have to establish your name and reputation. But you wouldn't have to start by explaining the very concept of what you are doing. There would already be at least some degree of familiarity with your kind of enterprise.

But Playback people have to be pioneers, and the more distant the host culture is from Playback-related practices and values, the more uphill your pioneer path will be. Playback Theatre must draw on at least some of these: a sense of community; an artistic tradition; an acceptance of the value of personal growth, and of public self-disclosure; collectivity; a respect for skilled artistic work that may not be materially ambitious or successful. A new Playback group begins to become established by allying itself with whichever of these elements may be present in the surrounding culture. That connection, however thin, will serve as a reference point until the work begins to be understood on its own terms. "Well, we're a kind of theatre troupe, except we don't do plays." "Playback is a way for people to share with each other, in a safe context." "Anyone can do this—audience members can get up and be actors." "It's a bit like story-telling around the campfire." In places where these reference points are too elusive, it may be very hard to build a performing group. In Japan, it's taken a long time for the people trained in Playback Theatre to begin to form companies. They've been more likely to use it in their individual work. A woman who trains telephone operators finds Playback useful; so does a man who works behind the scenes at Tokyo's Disneyland.

In New Zealand and Australia, there is still some sense of community and connectedness, even in the cities. When Playback groups began to form in these countries in the '80s, they found a readier acceptance than we had initially had here in the US. On the other hand, the public sharing of emotion meets more of a mixed reception than in the US, and there is less consensus about the value of therapeutic work. In France, the open exploration of private personal dramas is likely to be looked on with suspiciousness or outright distaste. The Le Havre group has had to reassure not only audiences but also themselves that stories do not need to be "therapy" stories; catharsis is not the goal. They have de-emphasized Playback's healing qualities and focused far more on the theatrical aspects of the work. It is most of all in this area that they can find a connection to their cultural context. This group initially came together through the theatre school, a well-established feature of Le Havre cultural life. More broadly, the existence of the school itself, funded by the city government, may reflect a climate in France that is inclined to be supportive and respectful of art and artists.

Ironically, Playback remains a redemptive form, whether you like it or not, whether you embrace therapy or not. The French group offers a means of expression and validation to the ordinary working people of their city. The workshop we looked at earlier led to a rapport between the often-divided subcultures of European and non-European French. In the intimacy of their rehearsals, deeper, more emotion-laden stories are starting to come up, and the group is searching for ways to fulfill them. Finally, most significantly, as the company enacts the audience's stories with increasing depth and artistry, the scenes become healing for the teller—and the whole audience—simply by being such an exquisite acknowledgment of a personal truth.

Other factors, unrelated to the host culture, affect the character of a Playback group. Bev Hosking and many of the leaders and members of the companies in Australia and New Zealand have been trained at the Drama Action Centre in Sydney. The DAC repertoire of skills and traditions have become mingled with those of Playback (a two-way process, since Playback Theatre is now part of the DAC curriculum). The work of these groups shows the DAC influence in its physicality and sparkling theatre skills with echoes of commedia dell'arte. These qualities also link the Australians' and New Zealanders' style with that of the Le Havre group: like Heather Robb, one of the founders of the Drama Action Centre was a graduate of the Lecoq school in Paris.

In fact, the features that distinguish one Playback group from another have as much to do with the group's own make-up, influences, and circumstances as with cultural differences. A group composed of psychodramatists in their forties and fifties has a different style, emphasis, and scope of activity from a group of acting students and artists under thirty, even if they are both working in the same cultural environment. The director's background is especially influential—his or her interests and strengths will do a lot to determine who joins the group, and the kind of work they choose to focus on.

In spite of differences dictated by culture and other factors, the groups I've described above, and many others that I can think of, are notably similar. They are all composed of people whose ages and vocations range widely. They all include a significant number of people in the performing arts and helping professions. Each group performs monthly for the public—in community halls rather than actual theatres. In addition, they all perform for a broad variety of audiences, taking a special interest in being available to people who are often cut off from artistic enrichment. None of the companies support themselves through this work; however, all three are highly professional in their commitment and their standards of performance.

A United Nations That Works

This combination of similarity and difference is apparent when Playback practitioners from around the world come together. In 1991, Jonathan and I ran a Playback Theatre workshop where the 27 or so participants included people from Japan, Belize, Germany, France, Great Britain, Australia, and New Zealand, as well as the US. There were also five members of the Playback Theatre company in Moscow, who had come at enormous effort, with no money and no English. (It was through the film they made of this group that the Soviet television crew, mentioned in the last chapter, had come to know Playback.)

The task for all of us, as we launched into the Playback work, was to find a place where we could truly meet and learn from each other. The challenges of the language situation alone were daunting. The English-speakers had to remind themselves constantly to speak slowly for those who were straining to understand, and to listen carefully to words spoken in unfamiliar accents and idioms. We had to be patient as the interpreter translated for the Russians. One of them spoke German, one spoke some French: we had to plan small-group activities carefully to make sure that Yuri who knew German was matched up with Johan from Germany so that between them they could translate for Valentina, and so on. It was very slow, but it worked and it was fascinating.

Soon we were freely acting in each other's stories, using mime or music instead of language, or enacting polyglot scenes that worked surprisingly well. We learned the flavors of each other's lives and cultures through the stories we enacted. The national identities remained, but the sense of barrier melted. Linking all of us was story itself, that basic, universal unit of meaning.

Every time we sat in our big circle, going around to give each person a chance to speak about their experience, I was moved by the combination of our diversity and our deep empathy for one another. The variety of voices and accents, some struggling with English, some speaking the sonorous Russian that by then had soaked into my eardrums, the faces full of receptiveness and humanity, the readiness to see oneself in others—it struck me that this was like a tiny United Nations, with the huge difference that this one worked. People here truly listened to each other and learned from each other. They knew beyond any doubt the potency of their shared creativity.

One more story:

In the middle of writing this final chapter, I take some time out to lead a two-day Playback workshop. Snow is deep on the ground, but there is a spring softness in the air.

The last story of the weekend is told by a man visiting from Brazil, a psychiatrist whose work includes directing a theatre group composed of street kids and longterm psychiatric patients in a huge city. He's new to Playback, but he's already eager to bring these ideas into his own theatre work. His story is about Brazil's recent long ordeal of corruption, narcissism, and greed at the highest levels of power, and the rage and disgust he himself has felt as a witness. He is not without narcissism himself, he says, like all of us. But his work is about giving, not taking, empowering, not exploiting, connection, not isolation.

In the enactment, two groups of characters alternately

take the focus: Paulo, with his theatre group of the forgotten, discovering their strength in the work they do together; and the monumentally self-serving president and his wife, as greedy as he is, and stupid as well. As the workshop participants enact the scene, their sense of story engenders some unexpected dramatic development. In their portrayal, Paulo's theatre people are the same ones that the president and his wife are exploiting for their own gain. Empowered by their work together, they rise up and triumph over the figures of corruption.

It is deeply satisfying to watch, and not just as the fulfillment of fantasy. Everyone in this workshop is involved in some kind of human services work, committed, like Paulo, to those in need. Our professional work is fuelled by an underlying, often elusive conviction that we can help, that hearing and tending to the troubled ones is a way, perhaps the only way, to heal a troubled world. Although in real life the Brazilian president's downfall was brought about by much more complex events than an uprising of street people and psychotics, what the Playback scene depicts is in a way even larger—the triumph of human connectedness and creativity.

And then there is the story of the story—the larger story of this moment, which has to do with our presence together here in this quiet room in rural New York, listening to Paulo's careful, precise English telling us about a part of the far-away life he has come from and will soon return to, different and yet akin to our own. His story mirrors the purpose for which we are all here: its theme is the theme of Playback Theatre itself.

Photo: Joe Murphy

*The original Playback Theatre company in 1979. Clockwise from top left:
Jonathan Fox, Vince Furfaro, Neil Weiss, Susan Denton, Michael Clemente,
Carolyn Gagnon, Gloria Robbins, Danielle Gamache, Judy Swallow. Peter
Christman with coat hanger, Jo Salas under the fishnet.*

Glossary
(alternative terms in parentheses)

acknowledgment: the stage of a scene when the action is completed and the actors turn to look toward the teller. See page 36.

chorus: the actors stand closely together performing choral sounds and movements. May be an element in a scene (also known as mood sculpture) or a way to tell a whole story. See page 40.

conductor: the onstage emcee or director. See chapter 5.

correction: re-doing part of a scene when the teller's response has shown that the enactment missed a vital aspect of her story. (Compare to transformation below.) See pages 37-38, 62.

fluid sculpture (moment): a short response in sound and movement to an audience comment. The actors build a living sculpture one at a time, each adding her or his sound and movement to what is already there. See pages 31-32 and photo section.

interview: the first stage of an enactment, when the teller tells the story with the assistance of the conductor. See chapters 3 and 5.

offer: the technical basis for improvisation. To serve the story, an actor makes an offer by doing or saying something to which the other actors respond either by accepting the premise of the first actor's action, or by blocking (rejecting) the premise. See chapter 4.

pairs (conflicts): standing two by two, actors express an audience member's experience of being pulled between two contrasting feelings. See pages 38-40 and photo section.

performance: Playback with a company of trained performers and a defined audience. (Compare to workshop below.)

presence: the performers' quality, when on stage as themselves, of attentiveness and concentration —"stillness and simplicity" (Keith Johnstone). See chapter 7.

props: pieces of fabric and wooden or plastic boxes that may be used for impressionistic stage sets or costumes. See pages 58-59.

psychodrama: a therapeutic modality also based on spontaneously enacting personal story. In psychodrama the teller is known as the protagonist and acts in his or her own drama, supervised throughout by the therapist-director. See pages 120, 122.

scene (story, playback): the full enactment of a story told by an audience member. See description of sequence pages 33-38 and photo section.

setting-up: the stage of a scene after the interview, when the actors silently prepare themselves and the stage for the enactment while the musician plays mood-setting music. See page 34.

tableau story (freeze frame, statue story): a story retold in a series of titles with the actors making instant tableaux in response to each title. See description page 41 and photo section.

teller's actor: the actor chosen to play the part of the teller. See chapter 4.

transformation: a scene which fulfills the teller's vision of a different outcome for his or her story, after it has first been enacted the way it really happened. (Compare to correction above.) See pages 37-38, 81.

workshop: Playback in a group setting where stories are enacted by group participants rather than by trained actors. (Compare to performance above.)

Appendix

The International Playback Theatre Network is registered in the State of New York as a not-for-profit corporation under the name Playback Theater, Inc. Individual and group members of the IPTN are entitled to use both the name and the logo if they wish.

There are currently IPTN members in the following countries: Australia, Austria, Bangladesh, Brazil, Canada, Cuba, Denmark, Estonia, Finland, England, France, Georgia, Germany, Greece, Hong Kong, Hungary, India, Indonesia, Ireland, Israel, Italy, Japan, Lithuania, Netherlands, New Zealand, Norway, Northern Ireland, Portugal, Russia, Scotland, Singapore, Spain, Sri Lanka, Sweden, Switzerland, Taiwan, Uruguay, United States, Wales.

For information about the Network or about Playback Theatre training opportunities, contact:

www.playbacknet.org
www.playbackcentre.org

References and Resources

On Playback Theatre:

Centre for Playback Theatre and Hudson River Playback Theatre. (2006). *Performing Playback Theatre: A training DVD.*

Dennis, R. (2004). "Public Performance, Personal Story: A Study of Playback Theatre." PhD thesis at www.playbacktheatre. org/Resources.

Dennis, R. (2007a). "Your Story, My Story, Our Story: Playback Theatre, Cultural Production, and an Ethics of Listening". *Storytelling, Self, Society: An Interdisciplinary Journal of Storytelling Studies* 3 (3): 183–194.

Dennis, R. (2007b). "Inclusive Democracy: a Consideration of Playback Theatre with Refugee and Asylum Seekers in Australia." *Research in Drama Education* 12 (3) (November): 355–370.

Fox, H. (2007). "Playback Theatre: Inciting Dialogue and Building Community Through Personal Story." *TDR/The Drama Review* 51 (4) (December): 89–105.

Fox, J. (1982). Playback Theater: The Community Sees Itself. In *Drama in Therapy*, Vol. 2. Eds. Courtney and Schattner, New York: Drama Book Specialists.

Fox, J. (1992). Defining Theatre for the Nonscripted Domain. *The Arts in Psychotherapy*, 19, 201-7.

Fox, J. (1994). *Acts of Service: Spontaneity, Commitment, Tradition in the Nonscripted Theatre.* New Paltz, NY: Tusitala. (Translated as *Playback Theater: Renaissance einer altern-Tradition.* Cologne: InScenario Verlag, 1996.)

Fox, J. (2008.) "Playback Theatre in Burundi: Can Theatre Transcend the Gap?" In *Applied Theatre Reader.* Eds. Prentki and Preston. New York: Routledge.

Interplay. (First issue 1990). Newsletter of the International Playback Theatre Network, issued three times yearly.

Park-Fuller, L. 2003. "Audiencing the Audience: Playback Theatre, Performative Writing, and Social Activism." *Text and Performance Quarterly* 23 (3) (July): 288–310.

Rowe, N. (2007) *Playing the Other: Dramatizing Personal Narratives in Playback Theatre.* London: Jessica Kingsley.

Salas, J. (1983). "Culture and Community: Playback Theater." *The Drama Review,* 27, 2, 15-25.

Salas, J. (1992). "Music in Playback Theatre." *The Arts in Psychotherapy,* 19, 13-18.

Salas, J. (1994). "Playback Theatre: Children Find Their Stories." In *Handbook for Treatment of Attachment-Trauma Problems in Children.* Ed. B. James. New York: Lexington Books.

Salas, J. "Using Theater to Address Bullying." In *Educational Leadership,* September 2005. 78-82.

Salas, J. and Gauna, L., Eds. (2007) *Half of My Heart/La Mitad de Mi Corazón: True Stories Told by Immigrants.* New Paltz, NY: Tusitala.

Salas, J. (2007) *Do My Story, Sing My Song: Music therapy and Playback Theatre with troubled children.* New Paltz, NY: Tusitala.

Salas, J. (2008). "Immigrant Stories in the Hudson Valley," in *Telling Stories to Change the World,* Eds. Solinger, Fox, and Irani. New York: Routledge.

Salas, J. (2011) "Everyone has a story." TEDx talk, www.youtube.com.

Salas, J. (2012). "Stories in the Moment: Playback Theatre for building community and justice." Volume 2 of *Acting Together: Performance and the Creative Transformation of Conflict.* Eds. Varea, Cohen, and Walker. San Francisco: New Village Press.

On theatre and theatre games:

Boal, A. (1979). *Theatre of the Oppressed.* New York: Urizen.

Boal, A. (1992). *Games for Actors and Non-actors.* New York: Routledge.

Brook, P. (1968). *The Empty Space.* New York: Avon.

Brook, P. (1979). "Leaning on the moment." *Parabola*, 4, 2, 46-59.

Brook, P. (1986). "Or so the story goes." *Parabola*, 11, 2.

Cohen-Cruz, J. and Schutzman, M., Eds. (1994). *Playing Boal: Theatre, Therapy, Activism.* New York and London: Routledge.

Fox, H. (2010). *Zoomy Zoomy: Improv Games and Exercises for Groups.* New Paltz, NY: Tusitala Publishing.

Johnstone, K. (1979). *Impro: Improvisation and the Theatre.* New York: Theatre Arts Books.

Johnstone, K. (1994). *Don't be Prepared: Theatresports™ for Teachers, Vol. 1.* Calgary, Alberta: Loose Moose Theatre Company.

Pasolli, R. (1970). *A Book on the Open Theater.* New York: Avon.

Polsky, M. E. (1989). *Let's Improvise: Becoming Creative, Expressive and Spontaneous Through Drama.* Lanham, MD: University Press of America, Inc.

Schechner, R. (1985). *Between Theater and Anthropology.* Philadelphia: University of Pennsylvania Press.

Spolin, V. (1963). *Improvisation for the Theater.* Evanston, IL: Northwestern University Press.

Way, B. (1967). *Development through Drama.* London: Longman's.

Other topics:

Fox, J., Ed. (1987). *The Essential Moreno: Writings on Psychodrama, Group Method, and Spontaneity.* New Paltz, NY: Tusitala.

Gardner, H. (1983). *Frames of Mind.* New York: Basic Books.

Hyde, L. (1979). *The Gift: Imagination and the Erotic Life of Property*. New York: Random House.

Johnson, D. R. and Emunah, R. (2009). *Current Approaches in Drama Therapy*. (2nd Edition.) Springfield, IL: Charles C Thomas.

Keeney, B.P. (1983). *Aesthetics of Change*. New York: Guilford Press.

Kellerman, P. F. (1992). *Focus on Psychodrama*. London: Jessica Kingsley.

Landy, R. (2007). *The Couch and the Stage: Integrating Words and Action in Psychotherapy*. Lanham, MD: Rowman & Littlefield.

Lederach, J. P. (2005) *The Moral Imagination: The Art and Soul of Building Peace*. New York: Oxford University Press.

Moreno, J. L. (1977). (4th Ed.) *Psychodrama*, Vol. 1. Beacon, NY: Beacon House.

Sacks, O. (1987). *The Man Who Mistook His Wife for a Hat*. New York: Harper and Row.

Williams, A. (1989). *The Passionate Technique*. London and New York: Routledge.

Index

Afterword to 20th Anniversary Edition

In a recent New York Times article on narrative, the writer Steve Almond says, speaking of a movie hero: "[He] is trying to do the work of a narrator—to make sense of his life, to divine the meanings concealed in the baffling world around him." It is what we all do, we who are neither fictional nor particularly heroic.

In a world more baffling than it was in 1993 when *Improvising Real Life* was first published, Playback Theatre continues to offer ordinary people a way to tell their stories, to make sense of their lives and find meaning amid upheaval. Looming climate change, the post-9/11 wars, the Arab Spring and Occupy movements, and the radical innovations in how we connect and communicate are all features of the new reality we share. We are linked up in ways that were the realm of science fiction until recently, allowing us to discover and share information at the touch of a button; to connect with another person, or thousands, in an instant.

Playback Theatre has changed along with this changing world. It has grown steadily, with practitioners now in about sixty countries and festive multilingual international conferences. Playback now has a considerable online presence, making it easy for people to discover and learn about it through electronic means—a vehicle that lives quite comfortably alongside the still-essential embodied experience of being in a room with others, enacting stories in the moment.

We've recognized and embraced the need for stories to be told not just for the benefit of the individual, which tended to be the focus in Playback's earlier days, but for the transformation of the group, the community, the society. The act of attending with care and artistry to the stories of real lives asserts something

---

[1] "Once Upon a Time, There Was a Person Who Said, 'Once Upon a Time'" by Steve Almond; *New York Times Magazine*, January 13, 2013.

bravely different in the face of immense forces determined to corporatize and commodify. It honors the stories that will never be selected for the media's bright lights and blaring amplification. Wherever people do Playback Theatre, small personal narratives of discovery, change, loss, dreams, pain, reflection, or triumph are brought to aesthetic life and entrusted to the collective memory of the audience that witnesses them.

In some instances this is an explicit process of addressing crisis or oppression, such as the Playback Theatre responses to the tsunami in the Indian Ocean, Hurricane Katrina in New Orleans, and the Fukushima earthquake in Japan; or the Freedom Bus project in Palestine, building strength and solidarity within a long, dispiriting struggle for human rights. In Afghanistan, victims of war have used Playback to give voice to previously untold stories, underlining their claim to transitional justice. In performances here in upstate New York with groups of immigrants, audience members find a public voice to speak of what they have endured and what they dream.

I've been involved in Playback Theatre every day of this long and evolving story, as a pioneer, a performer, a teacher, and a writer. I was very young when we started in 1975, and now I am not. I did not expect to be still doing Playback at my age, let alone still carrying equipment, sweeping the floor, and setting up chairs before shows and workshops. People sometimes ask me what keeps me engaged, year after year. More than anything, it's the sense of wonder that I find when a teller tells a story that evokes the complexity and beauty of a whole life, unknown to me until that moment.

I am also renewed and sustained when I hear about (and sometimes participate in) some of the Playback Theatre work that's going on in places of extreme suffering and turbulence around the world. It makes me step back and see what a powerful practice Playback has become.

Everything I do is grounded in the extraordinarily rich experience of being part of a long-lived Playback company. A few years ago, trying to follow the advice of yet another organizational consultant, we realized that we're not an organization—we're an organism, as are, I suspect, other Playback ensembles as well. Like the cells of an organism, we are bonded to each other, we are resilient, we adapt to change, if sometimes painfully, we are ready to pivot in a new direction when a new direction presents itself or is needed, we sense an organic force that impels our growth. These characteristics are echoed in our interactions onstage as we hear and enact stories together.

I wrote *Improvising Real Life* as a companion for those who are practicing or learning Playback Theatre. I am happy that the book continues to play that role, and that it is now accessible to speakers of other languages, with translations published in Germany, Japan, Uruguay, Brazil, Taiwan, Russia, and Israel.

I re-read it in preparation for this edition, finding, on the whole, that it still represents what I would want to say about Playback Theatre's basic principles and practices. By the time I wrote the book we had been doing Playback long enough to know clearly what it was: to have crystallized the roles of conductor, actor, and musician and to have established and articulated the integral presence of ritual. We were aware that Playback Theatre asserted something new or perhaps very old about theatre and that the accepted categories of art and not-art were inadequate for what we were doing. We had learned a lot about story.

There have been changes, of course, in some of the specific work I reported on. Nothing stands still: companies grow and flourish and change, or their life cycle comes to an end. Cultural and political developments have an impact on how and where Playback is practiced. Our actual work on stage, though still using the same basic forms and protocols, has grown in its variety and precision. Chapter 3 in this edition, "Scenes and Other Forms," has been revised to reflect current practice.

The original company as I described it in chapter 1 ceased to exist the year that Improvising Real Life was published. After our "retirement" in 1986 we continued to perform together several times a year until in 1993 we recognized that our time as a group was finally over after the death of our actor Michael Clemente. Playback Theatre in this region of New York is alive and well, however, carried on by the Centre for Playback Theatre, an international training organization, and two performing companies, Community Playback Theatre and Hudson River Playback Theatre. Several other companies are active in New York City, not far away.

In contrast to earlier years, Playback Theatre has a substantial presence in schools these days, from the Quaker school in Washington DC where every child is in a Playback group for a whole year, to a reading program for eight-year-olds in Houston, Texas, to my company's program addressing school bullying, now adopted by a number of other Playback groups in the US and elsewhere.

By now there is a considerable body of knowledge about the phenomena and implications of Playback Theatre. Others as well as myself have written further books, PhD dissertations, and articles investigating various topics, in English and other languages (though there has not been another comprehensive introduction to Playback). Some of these publications are listed in the updated References and Resources list starting on page 165. Curious readers will also find a great deal of information online about Playback Theatre, including hundreds of YouTube clips showing Playback in action (not all of it worth emulating, but that's the democratic nature of YouTube).

The Occupy groups in the US, forbidden by the police to use microphones, quickly developed a method that they call "mic check": those nearest the speaker chant her or his words, phrase by phrase, so that others can hear them. Then those listeners repeat for people behind them, until everyone has heard the message. It's exhilarating to be part of it—to use the unamplified human voice in this collective, subversive, celebratory way.

Sometimes Playback Theatre seems to me like a kind of mic check: we listen to a teller's words and we turn those words into multi-voiced theatre, so that a whole roomful of people can feel what's important in this person's experience. Then the audience goes out into the world, charged and changed by what they've heard, perhaps inspired to tell some of the stories more widely. Human to human; voice to voice.

Jo Salas
New Paltz, NY
January 2013

Acknowledgments

For this edition I want to thank Marjorie Berman, Roberto Gutiérrez Varea, Tanya Clifton, Elise Gold, Ann Belmont, and Lee Myer for their various contributions.

I also want to express gratitude to three constellations of people who sustain me in this apparently lifelong pursuit:

My students in more than 20 countries whose spirit of serious excitement inspires me;

My co-conspirators and dark chocolate aficionados, the members of Hudson River Playback Theatre, most of whom appear in the photos: Lauren Ardman, Dean Jones, Jody Satriani, Matteo Spitzer, and Sarah Urech;

And my family, in which Playback Theatre continues to be a central (if sometimes overwhelming) presence: Jonathan, Hannah, and Maddy Fox, their partners, and the beloved next generation, Ruben and Rio.

About the Author

Jo Salas, MA, cofounded Playback Theatre with her husband Jonathan Fox and the other members of the original company. She is now the artistic director of Hudson River Playback Theatre, based in upstate New York. She teaches Playback internationally and has published three books about Playback Theatre as well as numerous articles.